War Drums

Forty Miles from The Big House

War Drums

In the dying days of April 2015, in Baltimore Maryland, race riots erupted.

As world media focused on the death of one petty criminal and the firestorm around a certain West Baltimore location, what else happened?

According to the author, the riots were primarily a diversionary tactic by drug gangs to put police out of position, for purposes that can only be conjectured, and secondarily, to facilitate a race purge, that placed white residents of Baltimore City and Eastern Baltimore County under black mob rule for a full week, while every police resource was diverted to handle the mushrooming media circus.

War Drums is a street level memoir of the working class people of a town often called Harm City, who were publicly and officially abandoned to the criminal underworld by their own municipal governments.

War Drums

Edited and proofed by Danica Lorincz

Books by James LaFond

Nonfiction

The Fighting Edge, 2000
The Logic of Steel, 2001
The First Boxers, 2011
The Gods of Boxing, 2011
All Power Fighting, 2011
When You're Food, 2011
The Lesser Angles of Our Nature, 2012
The Logic of Force, 2012
The Greatest Boxer, 2012
Take Me to Your Breeder, 2014
The Streets Have Eyes, 2014
Panhandler Nation, 2014
The Ghetto Grocer, 2014
American Fist, 2014
Don't Get Boned, 2014
Alienation Nation, 2014
In The Chinks of The Machine, 2014
How the Ghetto Got My Soul, 2014
Saving the World Sucks, 2014
Taboo You, 2014
The Fighting Life, 2014
Narco Night Train, 2014
Into the Mountains of Madness: in [3 volumes], 2014
Incubus of Your Sacred Emasculation, 2014
Breeder's Digest, 2014
The Third Eye, 2015
Modern Agonistics, 2015
By the Wine Dark Sea, 2015
The Pale Usher, 2015
The End of Masculine Time, 2015
A Thousand Years in His Soul, 2015
Of Lions and Men, 2015
Your Trojan Whorse, 2015
White Wednesday, 2015

Fiction

Astride the Chariot of Night, 2014
Sacrifix, 2014
Rise, 2014
Motherworld, 2014
Planet Buzzkill, 2014
Fruit of The Deceiver, 2014
Forty Hands of Night, 2014
Black and Pale, 2014
Daughters of Moros, 2014
Darkly, 2014
Fat Girl, 2015
Hurt Stoker, 2015
Poet, 2015
Triumph, 2015
Winter, 2015
The Spiral Case, 2015
Hemavore, with Dominick Mattero, 2015
Yusuf of the Dusk, 2015
Mantid, 2015
RetroGenesis: Day 1, with Erique Watson, 2015
Easy Chair, 2015
Happily Ever Under, 2015
Road Killing, 2015

Sunset Saga Novels

Big Water Blood Song, 2011
Ghosts of the Sunset World, 2011
Beyond the Ember Star, 2012
Comes the Six Winter Night, 2012
Thunder-Boy, 2012
The World is Our Widow, 2013
Behind the Sunset Veil, 2013
Den of The Ender, 2013
God's Picture Maker, 2014
Out of Time, 2015
Seven Moons Deep, 2015

This book is dedicated to Boomy, an unsung hero of an unknown war.

Contents

Author's Note...10

400 Years In The Corn Field 11

War Drums...17

   Back to the Beginning..................................18

   The Purge 20

   Miss EZZ...26

   Harm City Watering Hole Factions 29

'The Flip Side' 36

   Oliver Responds to *A White Girl Tale*............39

   James on The Systemic Purpose of Police
   Harassment..40

'Chicken Wings en Malt Liquor' 60

Rooskie TV in Harm City 63

'Hunkering Down' 65

   Post Script 66

Bugging Out..68

NEGRO DAWN! 72

My Slave Pass 85

The Enemy, Of My Enemy, Is Still My Enemy ..90

   The G-Man Riot Scenario 91

Boomy Advises CSA Colonel James..................97

Walking With A Woody: 101

  A Limp-Dicked World..............................101

  Walking with A Woody 105

  The Commute..............................107

  Conclusion 110

White Wednesday War Drums 114

Hangin' With Jimmy L. 120

Mescaline, Quinn and Me 127

Post-Apocalyptic Notes..............................136

Breaking Crystal 140

Miss Ezz's Eye Candy Armageddon 145

'Rock, Paper, Scissors' 147

  Columbine Joe..............................148

A Baltimorean Asks..............................153

'Does the Curfew Make You Angry?'..............................156

  Managing the Slave Master 157

How Can the Police Be Strengthened?..............................159

'America's Microcosm' 165

'Not Here!' 167

The Harm City Lesson 173

  Assessing the Combatants..............................175

  Criminal Units..............................176

  Defense Forces..............................177

The Arsenal At Your Feet.................................182

'Sorry White People' 187

The Wisdom of Swine..190

    The RV 190

    The Cardboard City Crew............................192

To Neglect the Dead 195

    On the Stoop with Leroy..............................196

    The Dumpster...197

60,000 Dope Fiends and Counting....................199

'Man Down' 202

Reign of Fear..204

The Hate Train 208

The Hamilton Tiger Dance 213

Coming to Harm City..216

    The White Devil Says 217

    The Honorary African American Says 219

'A Time for Men'...226

    Stepping Into The Mangina Breach 230

The Return of Men?...234

Hoodrat Reading List..245

'My Peoples' 249

The Discipline of Stone.....................................253

    Class, Stoner Joe Says: 254

'From Time's Booby-Trapped Vagina' 258

Dialog with a Large Suburban Brain 263

A Darwinist's Crooked Slant on Society 272

The Wedge Formation 276

    Gear 278

    Skills..280

    Tactics 280

Author's Note

I have decided to retain the readers' comments from the website postings, as this felt like a two-way effort when I was writing it. The readers' comments really helped me feel my way through this as a writer. Also, the journal nature of this project is enhanced by the dates and times that come with the comment postings.

Thanks to all of the readers that helped me through this, including those who donated to the site as the purge was ongoing.

400 Years In The Corn Field

White Wednesday History: A Timeless Focal Point of Racial Disharmony, a Prologue to War Drums

Mondawmin is a West Baltimore mall and shopping center with a deep history.

The name is from an extinct American Indian dialect and means "cornfield." Before all of you guilt-ridden wussy white people get all misty eyed over the extinction of the local natives, I would point out that the process was already well under way. When the Ark and the Dove arrived in 1637, the Iroquois Indians of the Pennsylvania region were driving the Chesapeake Bay Algonquin tribes to extinction. The locals were primarily peaceful and could not wait to throw themselves at the feet of the Europeans in hopes of protection. These natives eventually intermarried with free blacks and have accounted for a significant minority of 'red bone' blacks in the area, particularly along old waterfront communities.

Fast forward 350 years to 1987, and the supermarket at Mandawmin, run by a Hebrew concern and staffed by mostly Anglo gentiles, was in the middle of a black-on-black war zone. Employees were robbed, beaten, abducted and raped by local blacks to the extent that the store shut down, and with no Korean family large enough to staff the facility, the store was not taken over by another outfit. Even the Stop, Shop and Rob ghetto food store chain owned by a black man saw the crime at the Mondawmin location as prohibitive to running a business.

All through the 1990s there was no supermarket at this location. Eventually, the company I worked for hired a lobbyist to bribe a senator for a tax break on breaking ground and make a deal with Baltimore City to provide uniformed on duty police protection paid for at the overtime rate by the retailer. Three employees I know well, Miss Ezz, Butch and The Mack Daddy, as well as Gorilla Wall Paul, made this their economic home. I recall Miss Ezz telling me that she cried on opening day when elderly blacks from the neighborhood, who had not had access to a supermarket in over a decade, literally danced in the aisles and praised the Lord.

Many of the stories in Harm City over the past five years have happened on the old Indian Corn Field.

Last week, however, topped the rest. While the cop and the manager were busy up front with a Tide bandit [Two at a time shoplifters load up entire carts with Tide for resale at bus stops and bars and make a break for it. To make matters worse, Tide is a money loser for retailers, who make mere nickels on a $10 purchase.], a man with a crowbar in his back pack crept back to the pharmacy, which at this hour in the evening, was locked down behind a rolling sheet metal door. He popped the door, grabbed some Benadryl and ran, making good with his escape, but was roundly criticized by customers and staff for not taking any narcotics. There is so much narcotics traffic in this neighborhood that record cash business is done after food stamps run out and 100 times the normal amount of garlic powder is sold per week, as it is used to cut dope in order to throw off drug sniffing dogs. If I managed this joint, I'd build a massive garlic powder display hung with sun glasses, fitted hats, triple-X t-shirts, and prepaid phones. Come on Mike—you want a bonus or what? Get imaginative and cater to your clientele.

The next day the manager was checking prices at the Target across the lot when he noticed a Tide bandit and pointed him out to store security. While he was away, a drama was unfolding on the first day of Free Money.

A forty-something ghetto mamma was in line with her twenty-something son and daughter. She was loudly screaming such things to her son as, "Nigger, I'm not paying for your fried chicken with my card—and your ass betta not be stealin' it!"

After a few outbursts like this, the cop was ready. Sure enough, after the lady paid for her heaping cartload of free food, her son followed her out with a double armload of fried chicken boxes; about $30 worth of the ill-fated bird.

The **white** cop blocked his way and said, "May I see a receipt for that chicken?"

The black man said, "Get out of my way."

The white cop said, "I need to see a receipt for that chicken."

14

The black man said, "I'm walking out with this chicken."

The cop said, "I will fucking taze the shit out of you!"

The black man repeated his claim to the right to free fried chicken, apparently secure in the fact that since Brutha Jesse and Brutha Al like fried chicken too, they will be sure to get him a big law suit against the cop when they come to town. He then tried to push past the cop who seized the chicken, which spilled all over the place as the black man cussed out the cop and went on his righteous way, assured of the support of the News, the DOJ, and the President.

When the cop talked to Butch, he said, "If I touched anything but the fried chicken, I'd lose my job and my pension. I've got two years left until retirement dealing with these animals—then I'm out."

And so the Corn Field remains, as it did for the now extinct natives, a place where one cannot expect to earn his living or trade with his neighbors, without some violent savage taking what is yours, unless there is a white man with a gun to protect you.

When the white man has had enough of protecting others, what then?

War Drums

Animosity as Usual, Forty Miles from the Big House: A Primer on the Animals Muzzled Up At the Harm City Watering Hole

© 2015 James LaFond

If you have not read anything written by this particular crackpot social commentator, understand that I believe in few things, one of those things being that you and I are slaves, and that the figurehead of the system that owns us resides in a Big White House south of the Mason Dixon Line, just as slave masters of the Antebellum South did. So please, as you marvel at my broken mind—at my strange belief that my M.D. State I.D. is a slave pass, and that the renewal notice that came in the male from the MVA, is a threat—consider that I have now been living in Baltimore Maryland for 34 years, that a year of that time has never gone by without my being attacked or threatened by multiple—and sometimes numerous—black men and youths, and that nearly half of those years saw me harassed or threatened by a police officer.

My crime, in the eyes of both of these mortal enemies, is the same, Walking While Working Class and White in a Majority Black American City.

I plead guilty.

Back to the Beginning

So despite the fact that I was drinking beer with four black men this past Monday, I was doing so ten feet from where, decades ago, three black men—one armed with a screwdriver fingered in his palm—attempted to pin me against a wall, only to hear the steel-on-steel ping of a 12 inch Othello gravity blade as my illegal, un-empty hand came out from under my trench coat in defiance of my white slave masters' laws.

As I speak with Hawk, a former boxer and retired mail carrier, Mason a retired cop, Dave, a principal of a charter school that stands mere blocks from the epicenter of the riots, and Sam, a towering 60 year old heavy weight who was recently pulled over and detained by cops who were searching for a 5 foot one inch, 120 pound, 25 year old suspect, they see me as a boxing coach, not a writer, and certainly not that long-haired knife-toting creep of the 1990s.

Among these men, who are an interview pool, I speak honestly only of boxing. In every other thing I act as a fisherman careful not to pollute the waters he plumbs.

I do not argue.

I do not inform.

I drop bait into the waters of their collective mind, seeing what it will bring. I do likewise with the whites I know. On Monday night, when I told a white liberal the truth behind the riots—about the purge—he got depressed and asked me to stop. Baltimore whites have more variance of group opinion and less variance in individual opinion, particularly where matters of race and society are concerned. On these divisive grounds blacks will hold a wider, and more informed, array of individual opinion, which seems to contradict the fact that they block up—in political terms—more cohesively. This is one of the reasons that I seek black opinions, the other being that they are less sheltered and have seen more, so provide more anecdotes.

The Purge

Our collective need to believe in a vast lie is so great, that even when an alliance of criminal organizations claims to be engaging in a targeted purge, we decide—left, right and center—to characterize it as a riot of the misguided.

I have been asked by readers to write a retrospective of the Baltimore Riots. I have no desire to do so. In fact, I am at the bar with Hawk and his friends nine days after seeing the first police cruiser burn on the TV monitor under which we drink, for the opposite reason, writing the prequel to the story that wasn't told, the story that will repeat itself, and, if our masters have their way, will likewise not be told. The story that has been told to the world was that of a black man being killed by white cops, and black protestors becoming enraged over the death of a helpless child of The State, and getting out of control.

The media narrative is of the riots. If you believe what happened in Baltimore in the dying week of the month of April in 2015 was a series of riots, than you have swallowed half the Lie, and its toxic roots are burrowing into your mind every time that psychic plant is watered by the CNN watering can.

The actual, true, narrative is of a PURGE, a racial purge that is a test run for a bolder stroke to come. But even this purge was but a diversion—I strongly suspect—for whatever drug land moves were made by the three criminal gangs—including the aptly named Black Guerilla Family—who incited the purge, which was read by the media as a riot. There it is, the narrative of the Lie, three steps removed from the real story at its inception and diverting from actuality on a daily basis, aided and abetted by all concerned, all of us taking a thought bath in our collective pool of delusion.

That is far from what happened. In short what happened was that the politicians, police, and organized drug gangs staged a show for the media. And, while the world watched a few square city blocks burn, the politicians rushed to cover their asses, the police declined to defend the bottom 99% of the population, and the drug gangs terrorized, and looted the city, which, I suspect, was itself a mere covering action for whatever drug land activity went unseen by their enemies in the chaos.

Make no mistake, we were treated to a magic show—or rather you were. While you watched the news, I was living in an open city, decreed by the authorities to be absolutely un-policed for the first 30 hours of Monday and Tuesday, and then from 5 a.m. until 10 p.m. through Saturday morning. I saw a total of three hours of news coverage with two and a half hours raw riot footage—the rest brain washing media spew.

The story I have tried to tell is a narrow, patchy account of the actions, words and observations of people who experienced Baltimore without law enforcement for nearly a week. My purpose in writing this prequel is to set the stage in terms of the denizens of what I call the Harm City Watering Hole on the eve of the last purge, and the next. A week after the wind down people have settled down to the new normal, which is no different in kind than the old normal, but greater in intensity. People have done their best—like good slaves should—not to let the recent raw reality affect their beliefs, and continue doggedly on toward the abyss intended for their extinguishment.

Hawk wants to talk boxing and could care less about the riots. He knows his people are easily incited to violence by their masters and he just shakes his head and prefers to discuss another recent disappointment, the Manny vs Money fight.

Mason is biting his lip, wanting to stick up for the police, as he usually does at such times. But the liberal principal, Dave, in his pink shirt, blue tie, and shiny pecan head, is waxing oppressive, going on and on about how understandable it is that people rioted—attacked their own neighborhood, put some of their own people out on the street and out of a job—in light of all of the video of police brutality against blacks on YouTube these past few years. Mason wants to smack this guy and shakes his head slightly as I egg the bleeding heart on, who also thinks it was terrible that his students—who did not take part in the riots—had to walk under the guns of the National Guard.

On and on, he wrings his hands over the oppression of black by white as I egg him, bringing up many examples from my own life of white cops abusing black men. Mason wants to throw up his hands. Sam is looking at me with suspicious eyes, wondering what this white devil is up to. Sam has been harassed by so many white cops in his 60 years that he cannot trust a white person. You see, he bought into the lie that the police represent the community rather than the government. Therefore, white police beating up blacks represent the will of the white community. Therein lies the disconnect between white and black in America, a divide that has been made more permanent and deeper over this past week.

Finally Sam and the Principal agree that the riots were justified because an upscale white man attending the Orioles game on the first night of the riots told a black protester, "Get a job."

Mason has just crawled down the escape chute in the base of his cop lizard brain as his friends decide that a white man telling a black man to get a job is just cause for a dozen deaths, hundreds of injuries, lost jobs and businesses—a burned down old age home...

Dave then looks at me and says, "I run that school for good children over behind Mondawmin, but I drink out here in Hamilton [I suppose so he won't be mugged by his Mondawmin brothers], and live out in Harford County. My next door neighbor is a racist redneck. We're friends, drink beer together and talk about the world, and he's trying to learn what it is like to be a black man in the city—that not everything is determined by race. What about you my friend, how do you see this?"

Mason groans and sits back, as if he is expecting me to defecate on the bar.

Sam looks at me from under his big heavy lids expecting that I will finally break out my KKK hood and dance along the rails chanting the N-word.

Hawk shakes his head and grins, as I decide how best to rain dark dread drops of uranium tears shed by mutated Iraqi babies on Dave's liberal guilt parade.

"I don't see this as black or white, but as slave and master, man and boy. Who is the hero of this riot, a black woman who slapped her boy—who kept him a sissy for our masters?"

Sam's eyes are bugging out of his head and the other mouths are open.

"I know two heroes, have spoken to them, and they will remain unknown. When two white women were being hunted through the streets of East Baltimore and Middle River by young black men, who came to their aid and saved them, but two older black men? To me this is about young and old, like that young buck that tried walking up on me on Monday night. Why, I ask, cannot the stories of these black men be told? I say it's because they are men, and being a man is what's truly against the law in this society."

I downed my beer, waved goodbye to Hawk, shook hands with Dave as Mason and Sam crossed their arms and cringed like visitors to a leper colony, and walked out into the sunny day, where only one young black man tried to intimidate me on the way home, as opposed to the normal three, and his dumb emasculated ass failed like the many hundreds before him.

Miss EZZ

As I entered the old plantation house—sorrowfully absent a wait staff in white livery—Miss Ezz called me on the Man Phone. This lady, who set off the alarm that a hood rat army was descending on her store after her cashiers told her their children were planning a 'purge' on social media, called me up on the way home to vent. She had just driven through the neighborhood where the adult support elements of the youth brigade were drawn, and painted a word picture for me that described succinctly the life of the kind of man that the Dave had decided not to be, and, as a charter school principal, was trying to keep other youngsters from that area from becoming.

"Well Baby Cakes, we're all back to normal in the ghetto. I just drove over to Eighty-three through my favorite neighborhood, between Reisterstown Road and Druid Park. It's just a couple of blocks. We had the usual twenty or so half naked males from fifteen to fifty, walking around, doing nothing. In the winter when it's real cold their numbers are about half and they'll have some clothes on. Any other time they're out here. If there was a job application terminal in front of that boarded up house, I could understand. You might see one, maybe two, crack whores. Today there was one Olive Oil looking thing pushing a rickety baby carriage along— without a baby, of course. I really want to yell out the window, 'Please, get a job!' so I called you instead."

Though she thought that she was just venting, Miss Ezz was giving a scouting report that would be of great interest to anyone that understood urban guerrilla warfare. Half of these guys are working. They're just not working for Wal-Mart.

Criminal gangs—or freedom fighters if you prefer— work as crews, cadres of fulltime operatives dedicated to undermining the enemy power structure. They maintain associations—as do biker gangs, and as did feudal lords—with part time operatives that can be called upon when needed. And those part-timers will want dearly to prove themselves for consideration as a fulltime operative.

The hard fact is that Baltimore is a war zone. The federal government has been waging an openly declared war on drug traffickers in low income neighborhoods since the early 1970s. In the late 1970s and early1980s three white men, who were relatives of people I interviewed, where beaten to death by cops in this war. There was no investigation. As the drug trade has been increasingly dominated in urban centers by blacks, they have reached into their community—as all guerilla forces fighting against an occupying force do—for political support, and have found it ready made. Now, when one of their soldiers gets killed, he's a martyr. This is a turning point in the drug war, which is being stubbornly pursued even as the rubble from the opening skirmish is cleared. Those half naked males that white conservatives think are willfully unemployed parasites, and who white liberals see as helpless victims of white conservatives, are the very people who will be running things the next time society breaks down into its component parts as it did in Baltimore nearly two weeks ago.

Harm City Watering Hole Factions

I like to use the African watering hole cartoon scenario for studying violence in Baltimore, not because it is ironically accurate, but because most of my readers have seen nature documentaries. The nature documentary filmed in Africa is probably the single widest shared example of predation study that we modern humans have.

What follows is my observation as to the general parts of the Harm City Watering Hole body politic. Little has changed in terms of perspective, with few people having changed a single opinion, but rather descending into unthinking emotion, which has had the effect of drawing these separatist lines more clearly. Things are largely now as they were on the eve of the purge, and as they will be on the eve of the next purge. Recall that the riots were the cover story, the purge was the central story the riots were incited to obscure. Beneath that central narrative was a subtext; a tale of criminal enterprise that we can only wonder at.

The social factions are listed according to the most proactive, with—in war gaming terms—the highest action rating, followed by those factions which are increasingly unlikely to act in the matrix of reality [for instance liberals typically mistake their thoughts and pronouncements for actions] and unlikely to react effectively.

1. Hyenas: Drug gangs in Baltimore are managing a system of association with at least three distinct levels of integration. They were the first and most effective to act on every level, their lowest level being the youth mobs of rioters.

2. Toothless Lions: City and County municipal governments and police forces publicly proclaimed and acted according to an elite enclave mindset, and showed zero interest with protecting individuals and businesses outside of the political elite, police, and corporate business structure.

3. Vultures: The media has fallen into the hands of the hyenas by circling exclusively over lion kills and vocally protesting any effective lion activity.

4. Jackals: Various left wing activists have pounced on the hideous carcass found by the watering hole—an elephant named Mondawmin, I think—reminding all, that the hyenas would not have savaged Mondawmin if the lions had not killed one of their clan when they suspected him of tempting their cubs with magic mushrooms.

5. Meerkats: The majority of the black population fail to understand the causes of the purge, and yet, are stuck with the majority of the effects, as they listen to the banter of the vultures and jackals. Although they identify with the hyenas in this struggle they will be increasingly preyed upon by them. In fact, the vultures have demonstrated an increased reluctance to report meerkat-on-meerkat crimes, paving the way for more purging of meerkats in the next event. Hyenas can easily convert meerkat burrows into their own dens.

6. Wildebeest: Conservative whites finally understand that the hyenas are coming for them, yet hold onto their chimera of a fantasy that a pride of golden maned lions will take over the Harm City Watering Hole and make it safe for ungulates—even those faggot gazelles. The wildebeest now believe that the lions will win the next round and everything will be back to normal. They rest

assured—albeit uneasily—that their hatred for hyena kind is now clearly justified. It is told that one amongst them preaches a cult dedicated to the belief that lions do not hunt wildebeest at all. But rather dine only upon zebras.

7. Gazelles: The white liberals of Harm City are in shock and dismay over the fact that the hyenas— having been preyed upon by the lions for these many moons—have struck out at the less dangerous inhabitants of their utopian matrix. They are busily looking up their collective ass for the blueprints to a watering hole where no animal is eaten by another, convinced that it exists, and must have been misplaced. In the meantime, since the hyena attacks, the general sense among the gazelles is that, if some particularly bold gazelles could get the lions to blunt their remaining teeth on their ideological horns, than the hyenas would be left in peace! Of course, once the hyenas are no longer under attack by the lions, they would soon learn to eat grass like respectable ungulates, and no animal at the Harm City Watering Hole would ever get eaten again.

Welcome to the Harm City Watering Hole, Yo.

Jeremy Bentham   May 8, 2015 8:33 PM EDT

Thanks James, you have provided us with another piece of the puzzle. Speaking of the War on Drugs, it is indeed a conundrum. Not only are we unable to win this "moral equivalent of war", but government mismanagement of its prosecution has caused more societal problems than it has solved, hasn't it? We lost the war on alcohol as well. The powers-that-be capitulated in that conflict because they realized that laws only work when most of the people in society support them. After 14 years it became clear that a significant portion of the American people did not support Prohibition. Likewise it appears we have reached a similar tipping point with drug prohibition. Those in opposition to drug prohibition either want to use dope themselves or don't think people should be imprisoned for using it. At least alcohol abuse has been reduced to a level our society at large regards as manageable and tolerable; could we accomplish the same with drug use if we legalized it? Our government has chosen to conduct the War on Drugs by ostensibly concentrating on suppressing the street dealers and traffickers; they have essentially been designated as "hostis humani generis" (enemies of all mankind) like the pirates and slaver traders of old. Although we lack the will to carry that sentiment to its logical conclusion, as our ancestors did with the pirates and slavers. Therefore, the drug traffickers remain undeterred, at large and in charge. The rewards still outweigh the risks in the drug traffickers' minds. Now, as you say James, drug trafficking has become connected with the struggle for "social justice" in minds of inner city blacks, which makes the conflict all the more intractable. On the other hand, we DID win the war on tobacco by not only restricting the tobacco producers (big, wealthy and politically influential though they were), but also by mercilessly persecuting tobacco users. The anti-tobacco movement succeeded in convincing tobacco smokers that if they smoked anywhere but under the open sky they were putting other peoples' lives in danger, even when outdoors, smokers must stay far away from decent folks. Have you ever seen any group of people as willing to accept their punishment as cigarette smokers? Of course, the anti-tobacco movement is largely an initiative of the Left (The Woman). Generally if a Conservative doesn't like something he doesn't do it, whereas, if a Leftist doesn't like something he almost always wants it outlawed. One wonders then what would happen if The Woman decided to persecute drug use to the extent she goes after tobacco use? At the very least, you'd probably see more people get put into a headlock, handcuffed and hauled off to jail for offenses that would

normally just warrant a ticket, wouldn't you?
However, it would still be the "asshole" police
rather than The Woman who would get the blame
for such arrests, wouldn't it?

Oh FYI James, folks in the inner city in my corner of
the country are talking about "The Purge" as well. It
is going to be a long hot summer for certain.
DL   May 8, 2015 5:41 PM EDT

Awesome analogies, razor-sharp analyses—-
nourishment for a thinking mind.

Thank you,

DL

'The Flip Side'

Prologue to the Baltimore Riots: Oliver Hayes and James Discuss Police Harassment in Harm City: Updated 5/13/15

© 2015 Oliver Hayes and James LaFond

I was speaking to Daniel, a concerned, upscale dude who graduated from MIT with a degree in something I can't quite grasp. He was asking me about the recent unrest in Harm City as he drove me across town, and asked me for a concise cause.

I replied, "The drug war is a war on the underclass, therefore you have an alienated and restive underclass—the police force is an army of occupation, an understrength army."

Daniel continued. "I can see what you mean. I ran in the D.C. Marathon last weekend, and the police who secured the route were all very polite, helpful, professional—until this one officer ignored a traffic signal and nearly hit me. I yelled at him, 'Hey, that's against the law! You can't do that.'"

"He then stopped and addressed me in manner that was chilling in its menace. Sure, he was only one cop out of the bunch, but, in his mind, he was above the law and very willing to impose his lawless will on a person of the class he is ostensibly serving and protecting. So I could well imagine if I were a low income kind of guy how bad it could be. So your point is that this is probably one of those cops active in—and therefore callused by—this war on drugs?"

"Yes, it becomes a culture. A culture does not require full participation for its norms to be imposed."

"Norms, which in this case constitute a culture of intimidation?"

"A necessary culture of intimidation if a small number of cops are to impose their will on a relatively vast underclass."

"Okay, so what is the solution?"

"I don't believe in solutions."

"I am sick of hearing that. You have named a concise cause, so name a concise solution."

"Okay, send me back in time—you can surely build a time machine—so that I can murder William Bradford and his Pilgrims when they land at Plymouth Bay. That out to nix the drug war and prohibition."

"Yes, prohibition was such a roaring success it is astonishing that we walked into this 'War on Drugs' so wide eyed. Thanks for the food for thought."

"Thanks for the ride Daniel, and please, don't mouth off to a Baltimore city cop—okay."

Just as the Baltimore Riot stew began to ferment, a few readers and I were conducting a discussion on police harassment in Baltimore. The bottom line on the riots was that it had almost nothing to do with the death of Freddie Gray, which merely served as an excuse to vent long developing hatred for the police force. The truth however, remains obscured by his plight, with the media only interested in examining the spark that lit the torch, without a care for how long the thing was soaked in flammable angst engendered by the federal drug war. 5/2/15

Correction: On one of the comments at the base of this article I mentioned that Charles was harassed by cops a lot after he shaved his head. He just told me that the driver for this seemed to be his snappy little pickup truck, and that, as soon as he switched to a small sedan he was no longer targeted for regular police stops, even though his head is still shaved. 5/3/15

Oliver Responds to _A White Girl Tale_

For some of Oliver's Harm City experiences checkout **_Oliver On Stupid Shit_** and **_Taking Out The Trash_**

Interesting read. I was expecting a little harsher viewpoint. I do disagree with it being a persecution complex. I have no misconceptions that cops can mistreat anyone, but what I realized, the older I became, was that it is different. At one point in my young adult life, I lived close to Belair Road and Erdman Avenue.

I literally could count on both hands how many times I left my house and WAS NOT pulled over by the police. It made me hate driving. These stops resulted in 0 tickets and despite my continued questioning as to why I was being pulled over, I can count on one finger how many times a reason was actually given. I always had my registration up to date, always took care of my car, I don't smoke and have never had a warrant. So the reasons begin to thin out.

I'm not even going to talk about actual treatment by them as that would take a book and based off the premise of the stop... well, it could only go up from there. It wasn't until I got older and moved to nicer areas that I realized my daily meeting with cops should never have been routine, and when it does happen, and I request a supervisor, I should actually get one. Just realizing how normal I felt it was [to be stopped by the police] when I was a kid shows me it's very difficult to understand the flip side unless you experience it, because in my case, I never even knew there was a flip side.

James on The Systemic Purpose of Police Harassment

You know, Oliver, I can count on two hands how many times I have been harassed by cops and on one hand how many times I've been given a reason. Roughly, this means you have been harassed by

40

cops about 100 times more often than I have, living in the same area, and honestly, I look a good deal more sketchy than you and have broken more laws.

Many whites will say, 'But yeah, James gets picked on by black guys more often than Oliver does, so it evens out.

It does not even out.

You have been attacked and threatened by black males roughly at the same rate as I have, as their decision to be aggressive is not systemically driven but makes more subjective sense and is based on opportunity in an environmental context. On the other hand, your mind bogglingly more frequent harassment at the hands of the cops represents The System attacking you—which is a literal order of magnitude worse than being attacked by a private individual or individuals. My recent post **_Jack Dynomite And Jillneequa_** is based on numerous real accounts from black coworkers and is in no way an exaggeration.

For the readers who may not know, Oliver and I have been acquainted through boxing and have inhabited the same areas of Harm City over the same period, roughly from 2002-2015. We have even had a cop follow us around in the snow while Oliver was driving me home from the gym—we supposed on suspicion of a drug deal—out in the County.

I have a theory that this harassment is all by design, as it feeds The System. Most urban black folks— who lack Oliver's insight, education, and experience in other environments—who grow up getting their asses kicked by cops just for being black, develop a deep resentment toward authority, laws, and the white community that the police seem to be serving. Of course, the police only serve The State, but impressions count. Terrorizing blacks causes tension between the races that justify the existence of The State as a peacemaker. There is also the fact that the black community generally refuses to help police, out of a very reasonable suspicion of animosity. This cultivates crime in that community, thus limiting the upward and outward mobility of its members and keeping them close to the centers of State power in subsidized ghettos, a readymade mob to threaten sissy suburban whites in times of economic woe.

This has a terroristic effect on whites, who cannot even imagine the frequency of harassment by police against hard-working young men, who actually

make up about half of the black male population—
about the same ratio as in white communities.
However, due to the abuse by police, a much larger
ratio of blacks practice violent crime, interracial
crime, and, most often, passive aggression, as a way
to set up confrontations. This behavior is planted
and cultivated by The System. 100 years—and
more so the further back you go—blacks were less
likely to seek confrontation and commit violence
than whites. Do not forget that the figurehead of the
KKK, Nathan Bedford Forest, considered the black
man to be a more peaceful and harder working
fellow than the whites of his day [even though he
did beat one black field hand to death with an axe
handle for challenging his authority], whom he
regarded as superior war-fighting material, having
led them to victory in over 30 battles.

It is now the other way around. For instance,
yesterday I boarded a bus loaded with college
students and working adults, all black; not a
criminal in the bunch. Exactly half of the seats were
full. Every passenger had placed their hand bag or
purse next to them, necessitating a confrontation or
a submissive request on my part. Depending on my
mood I might go right for confrontation by moving
the objects, which always causes a rush to move it

by the owner. However, on this particular day, one of the 34 people saw that I would need a seat and placed her bag on her lap—which is law in most mass transit systems—while most looked forward, stone-faced, denying my very existence unless I brought attention to myself and set up a possible confrontation. This is a working crowd of students. On buses packed with youths I have often had to physically move people to sit down.

Such situations for a person like Elaine—a white female suburbanite—are nothing short of terrifying.

The primary ripple this causes among whites is an aversion to vigilante behavior. Yes, I wrote that. Most whites regard blacks—who have been made passively and actively defiant through law enforcement abuse—as a predatory species. I know about a dozen white women who have been raped, and have declined to tell male relatives for fear that they will avenge them and end up in prison as the outnumbered victim of blacks.

Oliver, I see this as a cycle of cultivated fear that preys on us all for the benefit of The State. Even when the white cop who makes a miscalculation when dealing with a defiant criminal gets persecuted by the press, he is still serving the larger State, the Federal police, to whom local police powers are in the process of aggregating to due to these local events.

And I have a bone to pick with you, young man. When you don't show up for a training session and do not inform me by phone, the first thing that crosses my mind is that you are getting a shoe polish shampoo from a squad of Baltimore's finest. So, the next time you reach for your sweats to come to the gym and some vixen drags you back into bed, at least give me a text such as, "Hey James, coming up for air, see you tomorrow."

The effect I see in the white community is support for police violence based on the mob violence in Ferguson, and the fact that black on white violence is underplayed in the national press. In terms of The State cultivating animosity among social factions, any inequity on either side of the coin is a plus, with black and white animosity both beneficial to government growth.

The underlying driver is the opposing view of the crime-alienation process. In traditional one-race societies all you had to do to keep order was alienate or ostracize a person. In a mixed-race society this ideal of alienation loses focus. For instance, in white America, being convicted of a crime brings alienation. Your family disowns you and lets you rot—you are an undisciplined failure. In black America, being convicted of even the most heinous crime does not dampen familial and community support, as virtually all black men have been unjustly targeted for violence by police— black and white police—according to a century-old theory and culture of police work that is more akin to military occupation than to the type of rural policing that most American whites in my age group grew up with. Coming from these two opposing views of community policing, I see no chance of a shared view but continued divisiveness, which, in the end, only benefits the federal government.

I'll post this as an article and would like your commentary.

Jeremy Bentham   April 27, 2015 1:49 PM EDT

LOL! Well Oliver, James, There is obviously something about you both that bothers people on some level, whatever that common denominator might be. The police in particular, and when the police are bothered about something they act. It's just a cross you'll have to bear.

Based on what you are telling me James, the police in Harm City operate on the assumption that, with very few exceptions, everybody in the city is a "player", for anyone not engaged in criminal activity has long since moved away. Crime in the city has become so overwhelming over the years that Baltimore has in effect become a penal colony, full of either criminals plying their trade or social outcasts seeking a place to flop. Therefore, the police are corrections officers supervising inmates, rather than "peace officers," because there is no peace to keep. It scarcely matters then if the inmates in this penal colony resent the "screws" or not. Certain politically protected classes of inmates get left alone, but other than that, community support of the police isn't required. The only portion of the community left that still supports law and order are retail business concerns, analogous to the prison canteen serving the inmates (and providing what's left of the tax base of the city). We have learned long ago that cities with little to no business tax base left have to hand out a lot of fines in order to finance city government and/or obtain money through state and federal subsidies. So far The Woman doesn't appear concerned about most of the inmates fleeing the colony.

responds: April 30, 2015 10:54 PM EDT

You are correct Jeremy. The outnumbered police, awash in a sea of criminals, many of whom have never been caught, are not comfortable with men who are unafraid and also not part of the political/corporate hierarchy.

It is natural, and me being older, and more worn down by the years, am less bothered by it than Oliver. In fact, I am now proud of being harassed by police, and if they stop it I might complain like some woman who is finally too old looking for the waiter to card and feels like she has been cast aside.

Unfortunately this type of aggressive occupation style policing has gotten us to where we are. I don't know if there is an alternative at this point. For the cops to back down now will turn this into a South African style ghetto, as decades of these practices has forged a rabidly aggressive criminal class.

O Hayes   April 26, 2015 3:10 AM EDT

Baltimore is dysfunctional. But that being said I don't know of a major city that isn't at least slightly in the same boat. Atlanta, LA, Houston, Detroit, Miami at least are some of the ones I can vouch for having the same or similar 'dysfunction'. As for my appearance being part of the reason I was pulled over at a high rate, apart from attaching a picture and having a poll taken I'm not sure how to know if that's valid. But I will say 2 things, 1 a sketchy appearance should not be grounds for pulling someone over and legally it is not. It can especially be difficult when picking out 'sketchy' characters from different ethnic backgrounds. If I were an officer in Japan and I went off appearance to guess which people were yakuza I'm certain I'd be wrong 90% of the time.

A funny movie Harold and Kumar go to Guantanamo Bay satirizes this, when Harold and Kumar escape prison and accidentally drive into what they think is a sketchy neighborhood. The locals are playing basketball in the street, and a giant African American male , played by Lester Speight(who coincidentally is from Baltimore), grabs the ball and yells with dominance, which both Harold and Kumar perceive as a slow motion roar. They then attempt to make an erratic u-turn to escape the inevitable but they crash into a fire hydrant disabling their vehicle. Water spews everywhere getting everyone wet, and shorting out the local's boom box. So Harold an Kumar witnessing this and seeing Lester's character grabbing a tire iron assume a severe ass whipping is coming and elect to run on foot. As they run off Lester's character yells after them, "Where are you going? We were just going to help you change your tire..." at which point someone else rolls out a spare tire.. Lester's character ends up being a dentist with his own practice and no criminal record.

Just a movie but it illustrates the old adage 'don't judge a book by its cover' and I'd like to add especially if you're an officer and its illegal and causes more harm than good to the community that you police. It's not worth the 10% success rate to turn 70+% of the black populous against you. 2 if the reason I was pulled over so often was simply my appearance, then I'd assume I'd still have the same rate of being pulled over now but that's not the case. My appearance hasn't changed much but if anything I probably look more suspect now as I've grown a beard and switch between a bald head and locks. At that time I was pretty clean cut and no facial hair. But like I said, not much physical change to account for my current lack of harassment, except for a physical change of address. Now I still do get stopped or followed occasionally but it's not even close to the frequency that it was.

responds: April 26, 2015 9:27 AM EDT

For the record I'd say Oliver looks like

heavyweight contender Shannon Briggs as a middleweight.

Speaking of which, in Teddy Atlas's autobiography, he describes being with Shannon in a white area and having an entire crowd of white men attack Shannon on pure impulse. This was the day before the fight and Shannon would kill normal people if he hit them. So Teddy fought these guys off on his own while Shannon made his escape.

My favorite movie scene for police harassment was the first Rambo film, in which Brian Dennehy played a part that I am familiar with meeting from personal experience, often wearing the same type of jacket John Rambo was wearing.

I think what this comes down to is police looking for out of character or out of place individuals. Groups, even obviously violent groups, are avoided by cops in Baltimore, who have left me standing on the street in front of a mob of black kids that were breaking store windows and just cruise away, while they have also selected me and harassed me for being white and alone in the Baltimore night within moments of me being harassed by crowds of black kids, which, again, they drove right by. Yet they will single out a lone black man like Oliver and my employees. This all points to policing of the individual, of the State's sheep dogs herding us sheep back into the fold.

I think it is a simple instinct among loyal slaves of a system to pressure odd individuals into conformity. In some cases the cop is so totally off base that I get the impression that his suspicion of me—and some like Oliver who have shared their experiences—was based only on impulse.

An interesting corollary was a woman I coached last year who drives a sports car and is incredibly attractive. She gets stopped on average twice a week by Baltimore County cops. Think about that. Twice a week for 20 years now. And we know these stops are instinctive, don't we guys? Who would not want to talk to this chick? Well, the cops have an excuse to speak to her, as she is driving the roads that they police for their political masters.

Thanks Oliver.

Jeremy Bentham   April 24, 2015 3:38 PM EDT

Oliver must be especially dangerous and suspicious looking. Like actor Peter Falk (Colombo), who apparently looked so much the part of the stereotypical criminal type that he was frequently detained and questioned by police all over the world. I've see how that works myself. Likewise Oliver must resemble one of the actors from "The Wire" or something. He has hot looking women hanging on him all the time to boot. But he doesn't look like a user...Hhmmm. Yep, that guy must be dealing dope! One of these days we'll catch him holding. It would seem that the police are just being proactive in their own minds then. Like they say, Life comes to resemble Art more often than Art resembles Life. Especially nowadays, when people's perceptions and expectations are so often shaped by what they have seen portrayed on television and in motion pictures. It would appear Harm City is a particular pathological case as well. I have never watched "The Wire", but from my readings of reviews of the show I gather that the basic premise of the storyline is that everything in Baltimore is dysfunctional and everyone living and working there is compromised and corrupt as a result. Is that that an accurate assessment (of either the show or the city) or am I way off base?

responds: April 24, 2015 5:27 PM EDT

About the Wire, its reputation is well deserved and it is an accurate depiction of inner city life in Baltimore in the late 90s. The most interesting character is Omar Little [a composite of a few real killers] who is a homosexual hunter of drug dealers.

When we consider that any white man on foot in Baltimore, that does not dress like a preppy, a hipster, or in a suit, and is not elderly and/or disabled, will be stopped by the police about once a year on suspicion of drug activity, we have a start on understanding this. Policing in Baltimore is driven by three things in order of priority:

1. Qualifying for federal funding which means fighting the drug war and building arrest-based stats toward that end

2. Responding to news stories for

political reasons

3. Protecting major business like hospitals, and neighborhoods with strong business associations.

In other words policing Baltimore is all about targeting criminal males, most of whom are either pedestrians or are black. Like a Navy SEAL oversees the cop is looking for MAM [Military Age Males]. Therefore white men on foot and all military age black men are stopped as a matter of course. One year when O'Malley was in office 1 in every 6 Baltimoreans was arrested! Since they were mostly black males that meant that half of all black men in the city during that year were arrested! Oliver was one of them. No charges, of course.

I ran a supermarket for 4 years from 01-10. During that time I employed over 100 black men and just under 20 white men. I cannot recall a black male employee who was not detained or arrested on his way to or from work [even my elderly receiver who was dying of cancer. In fact I had three advanced cancer cases on staff who were all arrested for the crime of walking to work, with one of them being white. Two were named Jimmy, and they were all in their 60s and 70s.], and will estimate the occurrence to be three-quarters, with one quarter being attacked by other black men. Of the 15-20 white men, one quarter of them were attacked by black men and one quarter of them were detained or arrested by police.

This seems ridiculous, and it is. But it is also Baltimore!

I have some theories on why, also based on my experience with police and the 7 interviews I have now landed with cops—all reluctant interviews—and three with threats made to me; nice polite threats really—that being the most unsettling kind.

The BPD has no community support and is not sustainable by the Baltimore tax base. This causes increased aggressiveness in prosecuting the 'war on drugs' which further undermines any community support, for reasons including a resulting lack of attention to non-lethal violent crimes.

As any tiny occupation force does, the BPD feels alienated and outnumbered. The only East Coast cops who have it worse are in D.C. In the 90's five cops were murdered by individual black males in a guerilla war against the drug task force. Dudes would just walk up to their cruiser and shot them. It is well known among cops that few gang members and few men in general, will attack cops or kill the drug dealers cops are essentially tasked with defending. Those who do kill, and therefore pose a threat to police, walk alone.

It will fascinate you to notice that very few men in Baltimore will spend any amount of time on the street alone without 'packing up.' Those who do walk alone and do so with an easy confidence—as opposed to the furtive darting figure of the dopefiend—are not people you mess with, unless you are the apex predator—the cop. If the cops are lions than, to them, Oliver smells a lot like a leopard that needs to get back in his tree.

Incidentally, my white fighter, Charles, has been stopped by cops many times since he shaved his head.

Although Oliver and I are not violent, we are both generally alone for various reasons, not the least of which is we don't fear these goddamned hood rats!

The very same body language that comes with this attitude brings police attention. Cops fear military age men who do not show fear and who travel alone.

An interesting aspect of this, is Oliver's driving. Most young black men in Baltimore never drive alone! Seriously, it is so rare for a young black fellow to have a car, once he gets one, it's like an amusement park ride for his friends— a ho magnet. Oliver has been in business for himself installing electronics and contracting to cable companies since he was a teen, and mostly used his car to work, and to go

to Judo and boxing—not places friends
want to go—placing him alone in a car,
as a black in Baltimore, which says
drug mule, pimp, car thief, or hitter.

The cops are looking for the nail that is
sticking up. The white trash guy alone
on foot is considered a feral drug
scrounging beast with a warrant
hanging over his head, a stat waiting to
be tallied. The young black man alone
in a vehicle is obviously a criminal, for
he either stole it or is using it for
crime, or bought it with drug money!

I suspect we will find similar Trends in
places like Camden, Toledo, Cleveland,
Flint, those various dumps in Upstate
New York, etc. In the dying mid-sized
American city the old style white
laborer on foot or the young noncriminal black male motorist are rare
creatures and are assumed to be
denizens of the crimescape.

Thanks for the info on Peter Falk. That
is hilarious.

'Chicken Wings en Malt Liquor'

Listening In On A Bus Stop Phone Conversation on The Eve of the Baltimore Riots

9:15 a.m., 4/25/15, Loch Raven Boulevard, across from the Ravenwood Shopping Center

The man was in his mid to late 30s, dark-skinned, 5' 11, 185 pounds, and was wearing a purple fitted hat, purple XXL T-shirt, purple sweat pants, and orange and white sneakers. He nodded respectfully to me as we off loaded from the #55 and headed over here to catch the #3. He is a regular at the bar across from where I coach and was headed there for breakfast, I suppose. He opened his phone in response to a call and, as I sat and wrote on my lunch receipts, said, "Yessiree, I'm headed out to get some chicken wings and malt liquor."

[Ironically enough a Baltimore politician decrying the death of an innocent, unarmed, black teen in his mid twenties with an extensive criminal record, said on Thursday, "West Baltimore is about more than chicken wings and malt liquor. Apparently, East Baltimore did not get the message!]

"Naw, jus' me. Joey, Billy, Eddie, Sho-man, Sleepy, and Big Daddy all been barred from outta dat place."

"You know Sleepy order food every time out. Den, las' time he say he don't like his wings en throw his food at the lady—and his ass is barred out. Fool, 'Nigga it might be dat skunky piss you drankin'."

"Joey en Billy get in a fight ova the game—barred out."

"Sho-man break a bottle over some man's head. Went upside dis whiteboy's head with a bottle. His ass is barred foeva."

He politely stepped away while speaking about this attack on my declining gene pool.

"Eddie, his dumbass cracked Big Daddy on da jaw, up in Big Daddy's joint. Dat fool doin' a year. I aks Big Daddy 'bout dat en he says, "Fool got hisself a year ta live—then he mine.""

The bus pulled up and we were off to our respective destinations, respectable and otherwise.

War Drums

Rooskie TV in Harm City

The Skirmish Before the Riot:Tour Baltimore through the Leftist Lenz of Putin's Babe Watch

As this information hit the webzines a woman from my neighborhood was laying in a hospital bed with a badly bruised brain after being pulled from her car and beaten by black men in front of the police on Saturday night after the protest march, at Light and Pratt Streets. Her safety was not the concern of the police and her plight was not the concern of the world, so her story will remain untold, remaining a whisper, here on the fringe of the collective mind.

The story on this night was the loss of a Russian smart phone by an rt.com reporter and the interruption of the sacred baseball game attended by upscale suburbanites. The absolute lack of political and police concern for the safety of the tax payer was first demonstrated here in all its ironically Czarist form, and would go on to color the event in a dark gray, as the news crews proved utterly dependent on a police presence and declined to cover the majority of the city as it was systematically plundered. 5/2/15

http://www.vdare.com/posts/the-baltimore-riots-in-a-single-video-from-russia-today

I really want to be interviewed by a Putin babe—and swear not to rob her—but they went to this circus instead, as covered by Vdare. Since Baltimore is so close to the national media headquarters I expect the famously incompetent Baltimore Police Department shall serve as a boon to Leftist hate mongering. Actually the feds should just throw money at the problem and demand more unqualified and semi-literate people be hired as Baltimore PD, in order to maintain a constant status as dysfunctional police department poster child.

If you go to the RT article linked at the bottom of this Vdare piece you will see a woman in a shower cap. I forget her name but do believe I fired her for failure to pay for her "steamed scrimps" [a Harm City delicacy] back in 2009.

I love these phony riots as such media hate sessions draw the scum downtown and away from my haunts.

'Hunkering Down'

How A West Baltimore Grocer is Preparing for G-Man's Apocalypse

I was speaking with a former coworker who works at Mondawmin Mall [see ***400 Years In The Corn Field***] during his lunch. He said:

"Jayman, they done put out the word that they are lootin' Mondawmin as soon as Frederick Douglas High School lets out. These niggas are incredibly dumb. Hell, Freddie probably cut his dope with garlic powder he bought right up in here! After they wipe this place out they'll have to buy all their shit at twice the price at the Korean joint where them slope heads hide behind they protective glass.

"The Boss man is all but shitin' his self. We locked the shopping carts up in receiving so they can't throw them through the windows and are keeping the money supply low. With but one cop and one security I just don't see it. We lettin' all the white employees go before them hood rats get let out of they cages.

"Me? Shheeeeit, my old ass is gettin' the hell out'a Dodge!"

I spoke to a black friend yesterday who gets on various FaceBook, and tumbler pages and websites devoted to black ghetto culture in Baltimore. She told me that the last three parents that lost sons to the police have asked Al Sharpton **not** to come to Baltimore, knowing that he is a violence vector. She also told me that there is very little concern over the killings of black men by black men [which are about 100 times more numerous than killings of black men by police of any kind.] And that some of the thinking black women have become suspicious over the fact that when black women are killed by police or black men, that it is almost impossible to recruit marchers for a demonstration.

Post Script

The police ended up using this store as their operations base. One aspect of the police's defensive posture was the fact that they came to protect this shopping center, which although mentioned on the news, was not shown. Some of the employees are trapped in the store, unable to drive off safely as the police perimeter is quite small. According to the innocent unarmed black teens who planned the riot and leaked information to employees, their objectives were three:

1. Attack police

2. Attack whites

3. Loot

Ishmael   April 27, 2015 8:13 PM EDT

Big darkness come soon.

Bugging Out

Race War Rout

I have received calls from three people today working in city supermarkets who have had difficulty getting out of town. Gangs of blacks have been laying down in the street, laying bicycles in the street, and dragging trash bins into the street to form barricades. With the Baltimore Police department on the defensive and under siege by the black community, the media and the federal government, no Baltimorean is expecting an officer to respond to a call for help today.

This is the inevitable place where the drug war brings us.

For over 30 years, the black neighborhoods that have been systematically attacked by police prosecuting the drug war, which is their primary task, have become more violent, more hateful, and more expert in gaming the laws, coached as they are by law school graduates on a regular basis.

Noncriminal blacks are staying home.

Whites, who commute long distances to come work in the city, do not know the drill. The ones I talked to were warned by black coworkers that the mobs were coming, that the Crips and the Bloods and the Black Guerilla Family are joining forces to hunt cops, and that lesser criminals and even ad-hoc mobs of children are planning on taking advantage of the police being on the defensive so that they can attack whites and loot.

The key seems to be getting out of town before the schools empty, and gangs of children and adult-sized youths begin their rampage.

One retailer has flown in executives from around the region and called in all of the loss prevention store detectives to barricade the front doors of their most vulnerable location if they have to close for mob violence. I hope that gets really violent so we can see some video of actual fat white guys in suits defending a shopping cart barricade against ghetto savages.

I ought to call up Rick and suggest he play the audio from Zulu over the intercom! Don't forget guys, that U-boat handles make good counter-rams and that perishable shelf molding makes fair wasters. Since you can't risk taking the door pipes off the back doors, make sure your two biggest boys are armed with the cardboard ram you use to clear the wire slots on the bailer and the milk crate hook.

Strength and honor men!

It is, to me, finally refreshing that the lie of the police state is being exposed.

When only 10% of the population decides to confront and attack the police, the entire force is shut down, and the other 10% of the population that is criminal is free to attack the soft—supposedly protected and served—portion of the population.

The rub is that it is against the law to protect yourself in most instances, particularly if you are outside your home. The only reasonable chance a successful defender has of beating criminal charges is to have defended from within his residence after a criminal has broken in.

Freddie the Crack Dealer is being buried today. That settles nothing. Black Baltimore has its martyr. Soon enough the sissy white people that fled Baltimore and handed their neighborhoods over to criminals, and then thought that the city police would protect them while they worked and shopped and attended ball games downtown, will have come to realize that they have been living a spoon-fed lie.

Run rabbit, run.

Ishmael   May 2, 2015 3:21 PM EDT

Thanks James, glad I live in the timbered wilds of Utah/Wyoming border. Ordered Taboo You. Keep up the writing really enjoy it

JL **responds:** May 8, 2015 6:11 PM EDT

Thanks for the sale man. If it makes you feel any better I gave that book away to my niece. So your purchase will go toward her education.

NEGRO DAWN!

DOJ Stormtroopers Hit Baltimore

I am three pints into the riot and this is a first draft written directly onto the back end before I take my pre-work nap, so please overlook typos.

By 3:30 p.m., five friends and former coworkers had called me to say they had been sent home early from work because of impending riots.

The NEWS will depict this violence as a protest gone out of control. However, as of 11:00 a.m., black female cashiers at the Shoppers supermarket at Mondawmin Mall knew through social media that riots were being planned by high school students—an attack from students at one school [Frederick Douglas High School] on the very shopping center their parents patronized.

I knew this was coming on Thursday, when the Department Of Justice announced it was investigating the Baltimore PD. Take heed America, whenever the DOJ announces that it is investigating your local police, you will be hit with riots. It is the 'Go' signal.

Once all of this news came in, I headed down to the local bar to see if anyone needed a walk home, and then over to John's liquor store to check on him. Hamilton looked like 1980, not a black person in sight. The streets were deserted. Five cop cars flew out of Hamilton to reinforce West Baltimore and John looked at me and said, "Be careful. I am afraid. The police are gone."

I stopped back at the bar for my second beer and the news was on; the police passively defending against the students from one Baltimore high school. Think about that. One high school can press a mid-sized city's police department to the brink. Cops were driving in from neighboring jurisdictions.

I spoke to John, a middle aged gay white man who had his panties twisted over the prospect of picking up his 'friend' from the train station tonight.

Allen was there. His brother's wife was dragged out of her car on Pratt Street on Saturday night and beaten unconscious. She has a serious concussion. The blacks who did it were not arrested or sought as they are unarmed innocent black teens—the DOJ storm troopers who the cops may not harm as they are children albeit 200 pound children. Her attack will not make the news.

Only black lives taken by white men matter to the news.

The news rules us.

The news is our master.

To the news, the only death worthy of honoring is that of a black man killed by a white man.

No other life matters.

No other taker of lives is to be persecuted other than the white man.

You are a slave, and it is best to know how your master regards you.

Your master is the news.

If you are a black man murdered by a black man, you do not matter.

You can either be a zero or a martyr.

There is nothing else for you in the eyes of the news.

You are a slave.

If you are a white man, you may be a guilty bystander or a terrible enemy of the news. You have no other possible place.

Darin was there. Darin is a painter who was in a rage over the riots. He said, "This is not about police brutality. This is about fucking up who you can while you can. Just like those five black boys that beat me up last week, because I'm white and the cops don't care!"

Montrose, the black city cop, who is sitting next to him said, "You damn straight! We can't touch those kids. I lay a hand on a middle line backer headed to play college ball, I might as well have slapped a baby in the cradle—my ass will be in prison. Look, even the SWAT guys can't touch these people. They are victims. This is your faggot white politicians done this shit. Our hands are tied. The criminal is the hero."

I, however was thrilled. Usually, if I want a beer before going to bed in the evening, I have to sit there and watch Bonanza. I just said, "This beats the hell out of Bonanza. I, am entertained."

Montrose looked at me, and I continued, "Those boys rolling out the toilet paper are going to start a fire. If they find out that bags of potato chips go up like Roman candles, it's going to be a mess."

Montrose countered, "Shit, those fools is goin' to be eatin' that shit."

The other bar patrons, black and white, looked at me and shook their head. I had Megan call a cab for Mister Al, who is becoming senile. Al is black man who served in Vietnam. He might be senile. But he still knows lack of leadership when he sees it. He patted me on the back and said, "Jimmy, I'm a dinosaur. They will have to lay me to rest in the Smithsonian. But this stuff here, these two hundred police watching fifty young hoppers burn a car, that would not happen in my day. We might not have got along, but we believed in something. There should be an officer out there saying, 'Look left, look right, lock, load—and fire.'"

Although older blacks were bemoaning this turn of events, the younger adults were hiding indoors and only the youth were rampaging, and many of the cops were white. There was only one color to the rioters—they were all black. They have fulfilled their slave master's bidding and have shown the nation that:

1. Our Negroes are tougher than those Ferguson Negroes

2. That police are not organized in a way that facilitates protection of the population at all [and they cannot, for they are not a military militia, but a police force and policing is all about selective small scale aggression]

3. That soft civilized people are not the protected elite class they think they are and remain helpless before a mere mob of teens

4. That the Maryland Transit Police suck as bad as the Baltimore City cops say they do, because the BPD only lost one car out of two thousand and the MTA cops lost a car and a van, which is like 10% of their motor pool

5. That if Americans truly want to be safe from criminals, than they must invest in a massive federal police force. This may seem queer. But consider that the teenagers from one high school tied up the entire police force of a mid-sized city for going on 4 hours, even after the police received warnings and reinforcements from other municipalities. Imagine real adult unrest. Imagine thousands. Imagine guns.

I just got a call from an employee inside of the Mondawmin Shoppers, who is trapped along with coworkers, as the timid police use it for a supply depot during their defensive operation.

It is dawn in these United States, Negro Dawn. The federal government that fanned the flames of this race war did not lift a finger to help. They stand ready, however, to step in and take control, so that they can save us from their poster children, which we will be incarcerated for life for defending ourselves against. The janissary hordes of the DOJ are the hip hop generation of innocent unarmed black teens. For six hours now I have heard constant police, fire and ambulance sirens. You, too, could hear such sirens in your city, unless, you have large minority of Latino immigrants. The only answer to black youth crime so far stumbled upon in this great nation or ours, is to let a bunch of savage Mexicans move into town, organize, and then look the other way while they exterminate black males above the age of 14.

Oh, but that is so mean spirited and nasty.

Then run, white rabbit, run.

Jim Fry   April 30, 2015 1:02 PM EDT

James,

I extend deep appreciation for the street take narrative you've provided, along with your sophisticated / humorous / snarky style. Few writer's pull this off as well as you, as you parlay participles.

Having grown up in Detroit and lived through the transition from a relatively ok place to ghetto, I'm still left with imprints of watching the national guard troops and tanks rolling down the next street as they headed to the nucleus where various forces had kettled the then current black population of the realm.

What few appreciate or have been exposed to is that shortly after the summers of 67/68, the forest canopies shading and sheltering our streets were taken out via purported natural Dutch Elm beetles to provide better access for copters and monitoring going forward. We also don't have much collective wisdom remaining that race relations really went into the toilet in Detroit after the sweet community and music scene was nuked in Paradise Valley by an intentional division of the neighborhood by the I-75 Interstate being driven through its heart like a dagger. It is these sorts of subtle nuance bits that provide the genuine back story and allow us to unravel the woven myths and parlayed propaganda.

Critical Discernment, like common sense, seems to be in short supply.

Your writing is a gift. Thank you.

Jim

responds: April 30, 2015 10:24 PM EDT

Of course, James, and it reduced form, Jim, was the term for enlightened beacon of serenity in ancient Atlantean—a notably snarky language...

I'm glad you like the style and appreciate your info on Detroit, a place

I find of much interest.

Baltimore seems to have changed overnight. It is probably more akin to a scabbed over wound being scraped open, but down to the bone this time.

Thanks a lot for checking in Jim.

Jeremy Bentham   April 28, 2015 2:10 PM EDT

It's all part of the civil war The Woman is waging against middle class white America, isn't it? It's a low intensity, asymmetrical civil war, but a war for control of the country nonetheless. It's being fought on many fronts: in the courts, in Congress, in the state legislatures, in the county boards, in the city councils, in the government bureaucracies, in the schools, in the work place, on the borders, at the polls, in the news media and in the popular culture, as well as in the streets.

Ostensibly the grievance of the rioters is over the way young black men are being treated by Baltimore police. This is a highly ironic given that Baltimore is a 63.5 % black majority city and is governed by a black mayor and a black majority city council. Therefore, the Baltimore Police Department, in its interaction with young black men, must be assumed to be carrying out the will of the black majority of the city. If it were not, the leadership of the police force would presumably be replaced and policies would be changed, right? So what's the beef really? Where is the alleged oppression of black people coming from? From other blacks? How could that be? If the police are executing the will of the black majority of Baltimore, why are they not able to act with greater moral authority in suppressing the violence and protecting the community?

In any event, it appears that the end game of the "black lives matter/hands up don't shoot" riots is twofold:

1. To justify greater federal government oversight and control of local law enforcement. This will be based on the premise that the federal government needs to closely supervise urban and county police forces to ensure that they do not violate the civil rights of "minority" groups.

2. Black people will be given privileged status in their dealings with the police. The police will not be allowed to approach blacks based on mere suspicion of wrong doing or some flimsy notion of "probable cause". No more "black while driving". The police will not be able to be proactive in combating crime; they will only be allowed to respond to crime when summoned.

You might surmise that these policies will actually make crime worse in the inner city, and you would be absolutely right! But that is not The Woman's concern, is it? The Woman's solution to government dysfunction and malfeasance is always MORE government (controlled by the Woman). It going to be a long, hot summer then, like back in '67 and '68. The good news is that we have central air conditioning now, so we will be able to sleep with our windows closed and locked.

 **responds:** April 30, 2015 10:40 PM EDT

I see more poor whites getting squashed in the bargain.

SidVic   April 28, 2015 10:04 AM EDT

Someone sounds a little cranky?

 **responds:** April 30, 2015 10:45 PM EDT

Yes indeed. I was not yet done my pint of grog and had misplaced my Enfield.

SMART ASS WHITE BOY   April 27, 2015 8:20 PM EDT

Damn James, please don't go out in a blaze of glory yet with all this rioting going on.

You are one of the few white men that I respect out there that has the brains and guts to respond correctly to what's really going on.

 **responds:** April 30, 2015 10:47 PM EDT

It would be more like a haze of gory I think.

Thanks for the props.

We need more Smart Ass White Boys.

My Slave Pass

The Crackpot Author is Licensed to Work as a Baltimore Wage Slave Throughout the 7 Days of Limp-wristed O'Mamma Law

There is a curfew in Baltimore city after 10 p.m. for the next 7 days. Normally the thugs, bum-rushers and robbers hit retail and food service employees between 8 and 10. I avoid this by leaving for work at 10. This coming week, I will either have to fight my way through the thugs between 8-10—who will be reinforced by those frustrated over not drawing first blood against Whitey this week—or must brave the army of pigs that will be harassing me for being out and about.

I remember when I started working nights in 1981 and complained about being attacked by black thugs on my way to work, that an old grizzled grocer from the 1960s snarled at me while biting his cigar, "Christ kid, you got it easy. Back in sixty-eight I had to dodge bricks and bottles from the darkies just to get on my way, then the cops would be hunting us workers like we were escaping from Stalag Thirteen. Eventually the management wrote us passes and they let us on our way."

Remembering Cigar Face, as I stocked the frozen waffles, I asked my boss this morning, "Hey John, how about a curfew pass?"

He was thrilled, management geek that he is, went to his office, and returned with an envelope and smiled, "This is the first one of these I ever did. Thank you, sir!"

My pass reads, under the company letterhead:

April 28, 2015

To: Whom it may concern

Re: Curfew pass

James Lafond is an associate at Geresbeck's Food Market in Middle River, MD. He works the overnight shift and will need to travel during the Baltimore City curfew period.

Thank you,

John Stricker, manager

I hope to post 4 more articles on my riot experiences today. Sorry, I had to work over.

Herzog   May 1, 2015 8:38 PM EDT

Hey James,

I thought you might be interested to find out that you have a reader in Germany (who, to boot, even is a German, not an American expat).

Keep up the good work, and make sure you stay safe! I much appreciate and enjoy your writing and reporting.

Regards,

Herzog

 **responds:** May 1, 2015 8:45 PM EDT

Thank you Herzog.

My Father, Brother and youngest Son have all lived in Germany and have loved it.

Glad to have you.

James

Jeremy Bentham   April 28, 2015 2:18 PM EDT

Stay safe, James. We'll pray for you. I don't have to tell you to watch your "Six", because I know you are already doing that.

   **responds:** April 30, 2015 10:36 PM EDT

You know Jeremy,

Part of the reason I am so careful is that I'd hate to have to report to you that I screwed up and then have you quote from one of my own survival books the passage I neglected to remember!

I appreciate the prayers.

Phillip Alford   April 28, 2015 1:46 PM EDT

Looking forward to all of them. I have passed your blog site around to people who want to know what's really going on in Baltimore.

 **responds:** April 30, 2015 10:43 PM EDT

Thank you so much Phillip.

We picked up a lot of traffic this week.

I find this fascinating and surreal, especially when I saw CNN at the bar today and what they were reporting showed almost nothing that is happening.

The Enemy, Of My Enemy, Is Still My Enemy

An Analysis of the Teenage Thug Victory over the Baltimore Police Department

Black youths attack me and threaten me about 4 times as often as I am harassed by the cops. However, I count the cops as my greater enemy, for it is they who assure that I am unarmed and therefore as helpless as possible, before the youths whom they also count as their enemy.

The NEWS will tell you it was about human rights, the rights of a black man to not be beaten to death by cops. When white men are beaten to death—I've known a few—it has never been news.

What most of the horrified Baltimoreans I know have been saying pretty much follows Steevo's subject line from work last night, when he greeted me at the front door as if I had just accomplished some great feat by making it out of the ghetto to work, "Look, we know the pigs are brutal. They beat my ass a half dozen times when I was a kid. And when they throw you in the paddy wagon, they never strap you in—and then they drive like complete assholes! They didn't beat him 'cause he was black but 'cause he's a drug dealer that they're sick of locking up. Sure the cops are the enemy, but why are you going to burn down your own neighborhood and attack me because some douche bag cop beats some knucklehead to death?"

Many of the whites in Baltimore are somewhat to the right of Steevo, but still, the discussion stays in the feminine zone. The, "Oh how come bad things happen," hand wringing of the woman, which has become our national form of discourse. I prefer to look at things tactically, like a man.

The G-Man Riot Scenario

The drug war is being fought intensely in Baltimore as the BPD and various state and federal units ram in doors and run down dope slingers. Their enemy is a rabble of enemy gangs which rarely cooperate with each other.

Freddie was a dope-slinging foot soldier cut down by the enemy.

The major dope syndicates called a truce in order to take advantage of the media blitz over Freddie.

As soon as the DOJ announced that the BPD would be investigated for aggressively prosecuting the drug war, of which Freddie is a casualty, the Bloods, Cripps and Black Guerilla Family announced on social media that they would be shooting cops.

The BPD went on the defensive.

The three gangs recruited high school students to launch an attack on a major shopping center, during which they essentially fought the BPD to a standstill, inflicted more casualties than they sustained, and damaged police equipment and morale, while showing by example that the police are not well adapted for defensive combat, or any action against a group with mobility and/or numerical parity.

These kids won their battle. The fight reminded me of a battle in ancient Britain in which the Roman commander sent out his third string troops to fight the Bretons while the veterans watched and cheered. The BGF and other gangs did not commit a single resource and did booming wholesale business, while the cops were fighting for their survival against children. The immediate object was to open the West Side to a large scale infusion of heroin. The gangs made bank while the BPD got bloodied and humiliated.

The genius stroke here is the recruitment aspect of the riot. These innocent unarmed black teens will not be incarcerated for lengthy terms, if at all. Rather than the video footage serving prosecutors out for justice, it will serve the gangs, who will point to the most prominent rioters as leadership prospects. This is the reason for the camera posing and the frequent lack of masks. These rioters were, in many cases, conducting a working job interview. They just got 'jumped in by the cops' and have gone down in ghetto history and will use these films as training aids, trophies, and tactical studies.

This is effective opportunistic tribalism on display against the leftist Leviathan wallowing in the shallows of a sunken civilization.

The punks used flexible tactics and flowed around friction points.

The pigs did not.

The punks used the most effective mass communications network to marshal their forces, determine the deployment of the enemy, and then exploit their tactical successes.

The pigs did not.

The punks took risks and fought aggressively, with many individuals showing front line leadership qualities.

The pigs did not.

The punks were directed by aggressive, forward thinking leaders who have successfully destroyed rival gangs and killed enemies in battle.

The pigs were directed by a dithering woman who has apparently not had good dick in quite some time and is therefore paralyzed with the Sex Slave Paralex [To be defined in the next installment of Your Trojan Whorse].

This was a master stroke of operational planning that was so well considered and timed, that even the sloppy tactics of the raw recruits were able to accomplish the operational objective, which was to pin down the police force in defensive perimeters, so that over 95% of the city remained open for the drug business.

These kids need to be recruited to fight ISIL.

Let me reiterate that none of the 25-35 year old leadership participated in the riots as they had a board meeting somewhere while truck loads of product and cash were changing hands elsewhere.

I am not rooting for either side here but am essentially a leopard at a watering hole watching the lions and the hyenas duke it out. Ideally, there are maximum casualties on both sides. For the enemy of my enemy is still my enemy.

I'd say it stands as hyenas '1' and lions '0.'

May 17, 2015 2:01 AM EDT

Maureen

Great commentary.

 **responds:** May 17, 2015 10:17 AM EDT

I was not expecting this article to get any traction.

Glad you liked it Maureen.

Jeremy Bentham   April 28, 2015 3:35 PM EDT

"We live in a time when the strong grows weak because of his scruples, and the weak grows strong because of his audacity."

- Prince Otto Von Bismarck

Boomy Advises CSA Colonel James

In The Matter of His Restive Chattel: An Unsung Hero of the G-man Riots, Only Here Where Heroes Count and Victims Do Not!

This morning at 2:30, our regular customer came in. He is a 35-year-old Nigerian cab driver. He is always polite and enthusiastic about work and America. I asked him how it was out there as Bubba rang out his order, and I took my lunch break on the bench.

"Sir, thank Dear Jesus above that I am alive! I made good money tonight. People did not want the buses, were being targeted at bus stops. I was driving down Eastern Avenue into Canton and Fells Point to see if anyone needed a ride. You know, Sir, it is all yuppies moving in up there. The demographics have changed, and these yuppies cannot fend for themselves. So I was looking out for them, suspecting a need for help. I got to Fell's Point and the blacks were coming with sticks and bricks so I pulled out. Not a cop in sight.

"I headed back east up this way looking for needful people. As I was crossing Aliceanna, I saw ten black men with heavy clubs. They were about to cross the street. On the other side of the street was this blonde woman, just standing, wondering, waiting for the bus—a woman of the yuppies. I U-turned and pulled up, saying, 'Miss get in, quick!'

"She dove in and I pulled off with the blacks in pursuit.

[This guy is blacker than any American black I have met. I like his accent.]

"The lady directed me to her home at Highland and Fayette. When I pulled across Highland these fifteen black men wave me over to them. They wanted the blonde woman!

"I did a U-urn and screeched wheels, and they began firing handguns at us—boom, boom, boom! I thought we would die, but their fire discipline is as poor as their manners.

"I took the lady to a hotel, and we both thanked Dear Jesus above."

I asked him, "What is your name, Sir?"

"Boomy, Sir, I am Boomy—a Christian. What is your name, Sir?

"James."

"Well Sir James, I have something to say, and I do not wish you to take insult from it."

"Sure, Boomy, what is it?"

"Sir, I love America—your wonderful country—and am glad to be blessed in being here. But your mayor is a stupid woman that should be married off to Boka Harum, and your niggers, Sir—your niggers are useless and out of control, and need to be shipped off somewhere very far away from decent people. Good day, Sir, and God bless!"

It felt kind of odd sitting there after that, what without my horse, my saber, my field glasses, my bugler, or my six troops of cavalry. The beard though—the beard looked the part! I suppose, in my present impoverished condition, it shall take some time for me to round up and discipline my rampaging chattel.

I'll do what I can Boomy.

And Boomy, on behalf of the blonde woman, I thank you, and wonder also, if we had white men of your character living along the East Side, rather than 'yuppies,' would this even have happened?

Walking With A Woody:

Updated 4/29/15
In A Limp-Dicked World: White Wednesday—
Surviving A Nocturnal Attack By A Prime Buck
Looking For His First Whitey Scalp

I'm headed back out to observe the dysgenic soup that some hopefully long dead gang banger tagging graffiti for the Kaos Krew in 2000 nicknamed Harm City. Whenever I return to this place I will recount my experience surviving the bad intentions of one of Baltimore's aspiring race warriors, last night at 10:21 p.m. 4/27/15.

A Limp-Dicked World

This Monday night would be worked on less than two hours sleep as everybody I knew called me and asked if I was okay, if I needed a lift, etc.

I was feeling that I would be more okay than ever, as I knew with an absolute certainty that no police would be present outside of the sacral NEWS ZONE.

I could walk like a man, armed, with no fear of the government stooges I know as pigs arresting me for carrying a weapon in my pocket. Knife enthusiasts will point to the Maryland Statute and say I have a right to carry a simple folding blade below 4 inches in length. But when one deals with the cops, you find that you are going to get charged with some unrelated bullshit if the cops are suspicious of you and find a knife on you.

The cops are ever suspicious of me, walking alone, poorly dressed in a mixed race drug zone. Maryland case law is a murky, multifaceted, after-the-fact set of sometimes contradictory arguments that the most experienced judges in Maryland argue over, seemingly to no firm conclusion.

The result is that cops make up their own individual knife law as they go.

I pocketed a $5 blade and walked off down the way from White Avenue—the city planners apparently knowing, as if through a crystal ball, that this street would be home to militant Caucasian in the End

Times—down to Northern Parkway through the back streets. I love this walk as I have seen a huge—almost coyote sized—fox here on a few occasions. I also once woke up from a brief nap on my desk after passing out writing, thinking I was late to work, and staggering down here in my hastily donned work attire in a hallucinatory state, falling into mail boxes and shrubs, and waking up leaning on one fence with a dog snarling silently at me like I was the Devil.

This inspired my werewolf story Wake From Your Dream Place. I know this is kind of a tangent, but such were my tantric thoughts as I limped down the street, my left foot having been severely sprained grappling with Oliver on Sunday. I was, however, able to jam it in my boot, and felt it would not hinder me in a standup situation.

I got to the bus stop on Northern Parkway, just over a mile down into the bottom land between the ridge along which White Avenue runs and the ridge along which Taylor Avenue runs out in the county.

I looked right and saw nothing, no one. Not a soul had stirred this night.

I looked left and saw Tiny Dancer's brother enter his house, having come home from the eatery where he seems to be employed. No bus yet comes from that westerly direction. It was a fine cool night.

I heard a foot fall, a heel scuff, fifty feet behind me, and turned. A prime young buck stood there, having stopped in mid stride, when I turned to look at him. He was 5' 11" and about 210. His calves were thick for a black man, his thighs very well developed, his hips good and wide, his waist narrow, his chest deep, his shoulder rounded and terminating in long arms, the muscles of which showed through his gray sweat suit, and his wide head seemed pretty durable under the gray hood of his suit.

When I was his age I weighed 143. This is an old twerp versus young goon situation.

His hands were in his sweatshirt pockets. He pulled out his left hand and made a call on his cell phone as he stared into my eyes.

I looked around to ascertain if he was calling in support. The young muggers in this neighborhood go hunting with their smart phones, simultaneously looking for prey and predator; victim and cop. Most of the smart phone operating muggers work in groups of three and favor a run up charge by the large team member intended to knock the victim—usually smaller, or older—off his feet, followed by a stomp and grab attack by the follow-on crew, while the original hitter slides into scout mode looking for police response.

The night is deathly quiet. I see and hear no movement, including him.

I turn back to look at him again as he stands staring at me, his phone still held to his ear, speaking to no one, just regarding me with narrow eyes, as I suppose the phone calls out.

Walking with A Woody

I came to believe at this moment that he was marking me for a solo attack and was now calling for backup since I have made him. This is just assumption. But as soon as I made this assumption in my mind, I experienced a hard, throbbing erection. This never happens when I spar or compete, but does happen when I have encounters of this sort with young men who are larger or more numerous than I. I do not know what this means, am not a person inclined to self examination. I just accept this good feeling that seems to focus and calm me. I am not experiencing any adrenal effects and feel almost sleepy as I decided to get aggressive with him.

I shuck off my back pack and set it down behind me, in case some accomplice came up on me. I never have superior mobility against youths, so use my backpack or whatever burden I happen to have as a post. If they have to step on it or reach over it to hit you they are not a danger until they step around, and when they do that they show their direction of attack.

I don't like the idea of fighting with a hard on as my dick could get broken. I already have too much in common with Bill Clinton for my own serenity. This reminds me of the fact that I hate my dick—for various reasons beyond the scope of this article—which causes me to seethe a little.

He stands dumbstruck, watching my deliberate preparations for our coitus interruptus of an encounter.

I switched my umbrella—long and pointed but good for only one thrust against a big dude—into my left hand, where I intended to use it to threaten his eyes or, if his backup comes, to open up as a blinder for the guy I am currently stabbing or to shield against thrown rocks.

I reached into my 'please dad' ancient bomber jacket coat and palmed my blade.

He looks meaningfully at that now pocketed hand, looks back into my eyes, pockets his smart phone, turns, and walks away, looking at me over his shoulder every three steps.

I look around to make certain I am not being approached from elsewhere. When I look back his way a mere second later, he has disappeared.

The Commute

I have to wave the bus over, as he its not inclined to stop based on is speed and position. The driver is a larger black man with an insurance commercial baritone, who says, "Thank you, sir," in response to my thanking him for pulling over.

None of the five Mexicans are onboard.

Two of the 25-30 blacks are present. Both are extremely nervous.

I sit down and tried to nod off and take a nap, but my erection will not go away, and I cannot sleep with a hard on. I am once again reminded that I hate my dick, and sit irritated but enthralled as the bus driver talks with his dispatcher about routes closing, attacks at bus stops, the fact that all of the Baltimore County cops are in Towson making sure feral hood rats do not break out into the rarified white bread countryside of the white people that matter.

He drops off both guys, picks up one, and drops off the other guy.

When it comes to my stop, and I am off loading, he says, "Sir, please be careful out there. They're calling us in."

I said "Take care man, and thanks for coming to work tonight. It's a long walk."

I am limping now for two reasons—one good, one bad—and am irritated that I only have 20 minutes to make it to work lest I lose a quarter hour's pay and that I cannot possibly make a better time with this little psycho obstructing the process.

The lot of the Aldi's food market is unlit, which is unusual.

Not a soul is in sight.

The flag pole across from the park, where the insane fat woman sleeps on the bench, is rattling in the wind.

No one is in sight.

When I pass the liquor store I notice that the Pakistani owner has gathered all of his male family members in a vehicle caravan to defend the property. They wave as I walk by.

I pass no one else.

There is no traffic.

When I get to the 7-11 where I buy my condoms from the Nigerian guy, I am once again reminded that I hate a part of myself and am irritated by the slow pace. I walk partially for conditioning as my ankles are too shot for me to run. My heart rate remains in sleepy time.

Two local black youth emerge from the 7-11 with their purchase—chips, sodas and hot food—look right to see me limping toward them and then run toward their home, two doors down. I have noticed these guys before, buying dinner and returning to the apartment they reside above the auto-parts business across the dead-end street from the 7-11.

I have usually seen five county cops by this time. Not a one is in sight.

As I cross Middle River Bridge I stop and look around. No cops in sight, I toss the cheap blade into the river, switch the umbrella to my right hand and limp on.

Conclusion

As I make the lot, we have more customers than usual, and there are no cops randomly pulling over our customers and harassing them like they normally do. It feels good to have company concrete under my feet as I enter the store.

Bubba and Steevo cheer me as I walk through, having won their bet with Tony that I would survive Harm City and make it to work.

After punching in, I stand up front and call my lady friend to let her know I made it. She had been in a panic and had asked me not to go out, and to call her when I arrived at work. As I am comforting her over the phone, I see Nokia bending over in her purple sweat pants, getting the whipped topping out of the frozen food case I stock for the ambrosia salad she makes for the deli.

The lady on the other end is noticing I am distracted as Nokia smiles up at me, as I stand talking to another woman while blatantly admiring God's work as a chocolateer—the demon in my pants still screaming for a conquest.

Mom, I really hope you didn't read this. And if you did, I hope I'm still invited over on Sunday.

For my survivalist readers, the nebulous incident with the young buck seemingly out on the warpath, but possibly just some scared kid, who is just now telling his friends about this crazy old white trash guy he ran into on Northern Parkway, that is the reality.

The silent hand game in the pocket is where most encounters with possible enemies resolve themselves when you are not sure of his intentions but suspect them to be bad, and you hope dearly that whatever you have in your pocket is worth more in combat than what he has in his. This is why you never show your hand, never brandish a weapon. You hold the weapon in hopes of not needing it.

Later today I will write about my night out drinking with Mescaline Franklin in defiance of the curfew.

Habibi   May 4, 2015 3:08 PM EDT

Could you please edify the female readership on how it's possible to break a dick, since it lacks skeletal fortification (all jokes about boners aside)?

Sincerely and thank you,

Habibi

responds: May 8, 2015 5:58 PM EDT

Okay, it is called Peronie's disease, or something close. According to a late 1990s edition of JAMA about sixty dicks are broken per year. My doctor told me that his first operation was the removal of most of a broken gangrenous penis.

The band of calamari-like material that inflates and imitates a stick if your blood pump is still working right, is breakable, just like cartilage. According to various testimonies in the Clinton scandals Slick Will sounded a little less than slick with his 90-degree bent dick, which might have explained his dependence on cigars as sex toys. I assume they were Cuban, if not his man card should be revoked.

The dick can protect the testicles somewhat when soft—and is very durable in that condition. A hard dick is easily breakable.

Maureen   April 29, 2015 11:25 PM EDT

Oh my gosh. You and your penis.

responds: April 30, 2015 10:14 AM EDT

I'm working on deactivating the little prick.

White Wednesday War Drums

Second Hoodrat Offensive to Challenge National Guard and Keystone Cops

Last night, speaking with Quinn, a black school teacher, he told Mescaline Franklin and I that the gangs have been calling in false threats to city schools as far away as possible from the targeted attack zones so that the Baltimore School Police will be out of position—and they are!

My connection down at the Mondawmin Shoppers just called in and said that the kids are breaking out of Frederick Douglas High School and going on the offensive. She said, "The cops are shielding up and getting ready—there's twenty of them already in the hospital. I hope the guard can turn the tide."

As Mescaline and I surveyed damage in Hamilton this morning, we gathered the following intelligence:

1. The CVS, phone store and jewelers had been hit at 1:30 Monday night with minimal force in order to loot professionally.

2. Three businesses have boarded up to make it look like they were hit.

3. A gang scout, a prime 25-year-old crew leader or hitter standing next to me as Mescaline photographed the damage and precautions, was scouting for businesses that were pretending to have already been hit and calling in strikes for tonight

4. Inchon John, the Korean liquor store owner, said that yesterday at 5 p.m., an hour before Mescaline and I went down there to drink at the bars, five 20-25-year-old black men with baseball bats and gas cans were patrolling for victims, and that the one police cruiser avoided contact with them. He was frustrated that BPD police do not have the balls of Korean police and did say that one of his friends defied the curfew in west Baltimore and stayed

open, standing at the door with two guns and was not attacked.

5. My Libertarian neighbor is flying the American flag upside down next to a 12-by-12 foot sign that reads, The City Doesn't own you. Disobey the curfew."

For this bit of heroics, he earned free copies of At The End of Masculine Time and Incubus of Your Sacred Emasculation.

6. We are back to normal police presence in Hamilton, which is one car passing through per an hour, which is in any case ineffective on a normal day to deter crime.

7. Mescaline and I were questioned by unidentified-unbadged pigs in a large luxury sedan painted in dull gray. I think they were military contractors—all about 30, big muscled up guys with military haircuts and black tactical uniforms. They warned us to get off the street. Apparently they prevented looting last night, so will hopefully prevent the gang that is targeting the remaining Hamilton businesses. They were really sneering abusive pricks who hopefully get to vent that on some hoodrats.

8. The news is reporting that looting is limited to key areas. It is not. Professional, minimal damage break-ins to neighborhood businesses have hit every area of the East and Northeast.

9. Ambulance traffic in this neighborhood is at one per hour, roughly 20 times normal.

10. The curfew is only being applied to pedestrians and drivers passing National Guard checkpoints.

Jeremy Bentham   May 3, 2015 11:50 PM EDT

"Just drive down that road until you get blown up and then report back."

– General George S. Patton Jr., on reconnaissance troops.

"The white man thinks that because he sees no Indians there are none around."
- Indian proverb.

James, you bring up a very important point about the use of scouts by the street gangs. Winning the reconnaissance / counter-reconnaissance fight is essential to winning the main battle in any conflict. If you can detect and then destroy, thwart or spook the enemy's recon units, you can prevent a successful attack or, at the very least, minimize the damage the enemy inflicts on you. Insurgent forces in particular, whether guerrillas or organized crime groups, tend to be very methodical and risk-averse in the way they select targets and plan raids on them. Therefore, if they cannot case their target thoroughly, they will usually not attack it. So by being proactive in your counter-recon efforts you may even succeed in deterring an attack against yourself altogether. Well James, now that you have told us how to recognize the enemy scouts in an urban unrest scenario, do you have any advice on how to defeat or spoof their reconnaissance effort?

responds: May 8, 2015 6:17 PM EDT

I really wanted to slam my steel to boot into the spokes of his rear wheel, but then I saw headlines flash in my mind , James Zimmerman on trial for the road rash suffered by an innocent unarmed teen who had his modeling career cut tragically short.

I work on it JB. I have had a couple of countermeasure requests and will build a set of articles.

Its amazing how people outside of the military and crime do not consider recon. Talking to combat vets that's their big deal, that and movement. But most civilians just think it's all slinging lead. And, like you said, the crooks are even more risk-averse than a patrol in enemy territory.

Patton was such a hard case!

Maureen   April 29, 2015 11:10 PM EDT

Stay safe my friend. Thanks for the intel.

 **responds:** April 30, 2015 10:27 PM EDT

Look out for two things in your city:

1. When the DOJ investigates your police, expect riots.

2. Something I missed until 2 days in, was that the gangs send in scouts. Look out for 14-16 year old black boys on bikes and lone prime bucks with intelligent roving eyes and a casual demeanor.

Hangin' With Jimmy L.
At the End of the World, A.K.A. Tuesday Night, by Mescaline Franklin

Hanging in 'Charm City' with Jimmy L, nice and quiet out like the dead already dawned, and it's now after lunch and they sleepin'. Walkin' by I saw a young man of my shade (maybe a bit lighter even) wearing shades, a casual suit and a nice big black cane in his hand with a large handle. I had my stick with a few other necessities, and as I crossed White Avenue (don't laugh ya'll), we looked at each other and he smiled.

"Seems like everybody is walking with a stick today" He said without missing a beat(ing).

"I have no idea why!" I said with faux surprise, both of us laughing at the joke that the city we both were currently standing in was technically lawless. It was beautiful, sunny and mild with the spring buds in full bloom and proof that anarchy could work if only for a minute or two on a block here and there.

Jimmy L and I talked and ate and drank and talked.

Our first drinking hole was boarded up already in a sort of urban post riot camo and we returned to the fabulous 1920's (I wish) as we were now technically at a speakeasy with no password. After knocking on the door for a few minutes, a face of Irish (and maybe polish mixed in) extraction long americanized looked upon us with very suspicious eyes.

"It's Last Call, already."

The earliest Last Call in history, not counting when the Persians were finally conquered by the Towel Heads. The implication that we should leave was more than implicit and dare I say tinged with a degree of learned fear. A woman inside recognized the esteemed gentleman, Jimmy L, and soon we were allowed entrance to the bar from the not so classic horror film "Feast"(Whose star Clu Gulager once remarked of myself, Mescaline Franklin, that I 'looked like an actor'). Inside we were allowed one beer and it felt apocalyptical and surreal with no day light coming through the one window In the joint, boarded up to resist the savage hordes of cop-destroying high school kids.

Inside everyone seemed a bit subdued but I enjoyed the time, the End of the World fetish, punctuated by some senile black pastor talking typical social justice nonsense mixed with scripture (oh wait, it is one and the same, hence my anti-theism, which includes atheism as the most hated of religions). I was like, "Who is this fool?"

Some worthless asshole gets his chicken neck or back or whatever snapped by pigs (some animals are more Equal than others) and people have a right to destroy things?

Actually they do, not because of the injustice (of which there is none) but because THEY COULD.

They took the moment and imposed their wills and kicked the crap out of the pigs who make you and I nod, put our hands where they can see em and prevent us from defending ourselves. No Justice, No

Peace is actually quite accurate, although chanted by mindless hordes. Right for the Wrong reason.

There is no Justice only strength or weakness.

There is no Peace, only a lull in the war we call life.

Anyhow, we ended the night at the hipster bar across the street which was packed with hipsters, even one or two of their children, some lesbians and some gay guys. Jimmy L, Me and Mister Quinn, who could not get a drink at The Worlds End pub, sat and talked and drank, 80's new romantic music in the background. The ever astute Jimmy L noticed the difference between the Happy Hipster and The World's End Pub.

The smart and beautiful people were not afraid although few of them could probably defend themselves at all from savage youth attacks. Meanwhile the tougher and weathered working class was bugging out early. Was this a turn on its head, dialectical moment at the end of history?

Nah, son. It was one group that has been hammered between the pigs and the savages for so long, it was like a beaten dog, cringing. The beautiful people across the street (And some were, I won't lie) were confident that they would be safe. Apparently never knowing a sucker punch from a youth or getting a fat cop finger put in your face.

Like the SWPL saying goes, "there is no unhappy ending."

Five drinks or so later, we were the last ones at the bar and soon the owner asked us to leave, looking at us with both disdain and slight trepidation. Hey, we made that place more interesting, pal! The wait staff there are really cool however and I wish them luck and safety till next we meet. Same with the staff across the street. My dwindling faith in humanity, both hipster and proletariat is challenged by these good people. So we left and were technically law breakers the second we opened the door and set foot out onto the sidewalk.

The Curfew.

We walked off into the quiet night, beautiful and moonlit. A night for dark spirits to work their magic and the lunar goddess watching us and hoping her cousin the comet would come visit and wipe out these disgusting primates. But not tonight, sadly.

Not a minute down the avenue, a grey umarked paid for by joe sap taxpayer pulled alongside us and asked us in that condescending and I-hope-you-give-us-a-problem-so-we-can-fuck-you-up tone. Being 'Cauks'(as per Tito Perdue), we would not be avenged or cared for. After answering diligently and with full compliance, we were allowed on our way to roam back to a safe place to lay our heads. And still, the restless call of a moonlit night lead to another beer and sitting on the porch.

As American as it gets. Jimmy L counted the cars that went by and noticed this was a pedestrian curfew only. The first one for adults he could remember since the Gipper Administration. Despite his sage stage and wizened years, I suspected no senility and took him for his word.

Good luck with your pass, tonight! Remember to show your papers.

It was fun and surreal. One imagines five years from now. The Iron Masked Lady with the slowly melting face is up next for eight years. The gynocentric wheel is turning ever so more and it's what this place deserves. Womanly men and women who act like womanly men and the hordes who are separated by an ever thinning wall of cannon fodder whites, soon to be Mestizos (they hope) as Arabs did of their Turkish 'servants'.

Mescaline, Quinn and Me
Conversing with a Visiting Radical Right Winger and Black Urban Educator Just before Curfew in Harm City

When the news went out to the world that Harm City was erupting in riots, I received a call from an unlikely tourist; a young man spawned, twisted and tempered in the forge of another east coast dump, Camden, New Jersey, a city policed by the U.S. Marshals. My white nationalist friend Mescaline Franklin said, "Jim, I'd like to sit and have a beer with you while we watch the den of iniquity burn."

So there we were, seeing my friend Quinn as he stepped off the bus. Quinn is a 59 year old liberal democrat black Baltimore City teacher. Oddly enough, Mescaline and Quinn like each other's

127

company. When Quinn gets off the bus Mescaline says, "That's the guy—the GQ mugging guy. Let's buy him a beer."

We had just seen someone go into the mixed-race sports bar, yet Quinn could not get in. We stepped up and he said, "Maybe they'll let me in if I'm with you people."

We knocked and knocked, but no one answered. Quinn then said, "I guess not."

As he walked off dejectedly the door opened and they let us in for last call. Half the bar was black and half white. They did not want Quinn in there because he had gotten into an argument about the riots with two white patrons yesterday.

We drank our beer while two large women pawed Mescaline's bare tattooed shoulders and biceps, the super large one purring in her throat as she playfully snarled, "I need someone to protect me, and I see that protection happening behind closed doors, baby. She then tapped me with the back of hand too, and chortled, "You too honey. My old man will understand!"

After hastily downing our brews we were back on the street and Quinn was standing shaking his head. Mescaline said, "We need to cheer him up, buy him a beer—a sorry excuse for a racist I am!"

Quinn, only a part time teacher who has been losing hours at work due to the unrest despaired of going across the street to the upscale bar. But Mescaline put one muscular arm over his shoulder and declared, "It's on me brother, come on."

Quinn, sighed with a slight note of protest, "Brother—you better be careful saying that around these hockey fans."

Mescaline was dismissive, "Nah, all of them have been beat up by the cops and the blacks, so they're on edge. Let's go drink with these faggot hipsters. The wait staff is real nice."

As we entered the bar, Quinn was wowed by the real feel of the place, although he was put off by the upscale beer selection. He settled for National Boh and we settled into a three-hour conversation that went all over the place, from Quinn being stalked by two black youths and avoiding their attention by taking the wrong bus and cruising all the way across town to avoid an attack. They, like him, were black, of course. And he was well aware that if they killed him he would not be regarded as worth a news bite, let alone a protest.

Used to liberal-conservative discourse, Quinn was quite fascinated by the Darwinism of LaFond and the ethno-anarchy stance of Mescaline. We sat next to a pillar on three stools around a one by two foot beer stand, with Quinn in the middle. Quinn would alternately be drawn in magnetically toward Mescaline's novel political discourse, and repelled by the younger man's hyper angst body language. For instance, when he makes a certain point he seems to be crushing a small enemy skull as he looks into its eyes.

At one juncture, Quinn, said, "What about the curfew? How do we get home?"

I responded, "Why do you think we are buying you drinks? You are the sacrificial lamb we will throw to the pigs when they come with their truncheons!"

Quinn made wide eyes and said, "With all due respect, among the three of us, I would venture to say that I am the most respectable looking by far. Over here we have a heavy from a b-movie. And you

Mister LaFond, have perfected the abrasive white trash persona to a T!"

After a good laugh and more beer, Quinn asked me what my next piece was which I had outlined, and I said, "I am going to write a piece on why our mayor would make better decisions if she was my sex slave."

Mescaline chimed in, "You know, even though it goes against my evil racist creedo, I am attracted to your Mulattress-in-Chief."

Quinn and expert on such things, waxed physiognomic, "It's the lips, she has those lovely lips because she used to be a fat girl."

I agreed, "That could explain my Clintonesque fixation."

Quinn: "Really Sheila Dixon was the girl—corrupt as shit, but a hot momma—had that sway to her walk."

Mescaline: "Oh, really, a corrupt black politician in a mid-sized American city? I don't believe it."

Quinn: "I need to take you across the street sometime to educate those thick-headed cousins of yours!"

James: "Steela Dixon is what we called the former ebony babe-mayor. A prime ghetto queen—could be the villainess in a hip-hop movie."

Quinn: "Yes, but at least she had that presence. I remember sitting at a City Council hearing, that was concerned with, among other things, my job. This was back when Ms. Rollings-Blake was on the City Council. At a certain point—and this was when she was a big girl—she sent her assistant out to get a bucket of KFC fried chicken, and sat in the corner and ate the whole thing. Really? That's where she comes from. So perhaps you'd have a point about her being a dominance-starved sex slave joined at the hip with some hyphenated yes-man. Still, Sheila Dixon in a heartbeat."

James: "Me, all have to go with the underused former fat girl."

Quinn: "What about you Mister Franklin, what kind of woman is to your taste?"

Mescaline: "You see, I'm a white-identified guy. So I won't let myself cross that line. And, tragically, the only women who smile at me are black and Latina. Now, and this is embarrassing, the kind of women I am attracted to, are these kind of women, the hipster chicks in here that hang out with these gay liberals and have no fear of the police goon squad because the entire system is built around worshipping them and catering to their despicable sensibilities. I am attracted to them, yet hate who they are."

Quinn: "Before I can even begin to wrap my head around that, I will need another beer."

Mescaline: "Amen brother, make it a double."

Quinn than looked out the window and up into the sky as if imagining another time. "I lived through the sixty-eight riots. This almost does not deserve the term. Back then you had militant men bringing pictures of Doctor King to business owners. And if you hung that picture in your window you were spared. This time around—it's about stealing tennis shoes. Something has been lost—some substance that slipped through our fingers."

Riley   April 29, 2015 8:35 PM EDT

You write well, and are generous to put out the good reporting you do. I haven't been in big cities for years, so it's exotic in a way. I have some connections to Baltimore but most moved. I did live in New Orleans for twenty five years or so.

Thanks also for your combat writing. Being aged, I tend towards a good reliable firearm and can shoot. Still, one needs more than one trick.

I live at altitude and most of my neighbors are animals. I admire your fortitude and think I might see why you do it, but I don't envy you. Good luck in the coming changes.

 **responds:** April 30, 2015 10:34 PM EDT

Living at altitude with animals?

You mean they still have high rise projects somewhere in the U.S., Riley? I thought the housing subsidies were being dispersed to increase suburban sprawl?

Seriously, I suppose this is my wilderness. On Monday night, I felt like Daniel Boone ignoring a British order to stay on the east side of the divide.

Thanks a lot for supporting the site.

Post-Apocalyptic Notes
A Pedestrian's View of the Aftermath and Curfew

I have not seen a single frame of news nor heard a single sound bite. I have time only for working, writing, training and traveling.

Last night I took the bus from Towson, the seat of Northern Baltimore County, which was saturated with police coverage. This is the choke point where the police have gathered to stop the hood rats from hitting the white people who matter. Police coverage was 5 times normal.

The bus was at half capacity. These riders, and everyone I met through the night, other than Columbine Joe, were in a deep funk. The mood was precisely that following a World Series or Super Bowl loss. Some of the men my age were close to tears as they mumbled about the riots. Where the

136

mood on Monday and Tuesday was that morbid pre-hurricane sense of impending doom, last night's mood had nothing but despair about it.

As the bus dips into the city for three miles, I note a total of five pedestrians waiting at stops, 4 young women and one old man, all black. No military age males are in sight. There is zero police coverage. I would normally see two cars and a chopper. There was nothing.

Western Baltimore County was just as empty with no military age males and only two girls. There was zero police coverage. I normally see five cruisers and saw none. I walked to work with the only character out and about, a guy by the name of Columbine Joe who will get his own Harm City tag later today. Last night netted me material for 31 stories, and I'll see how many I can post before I have to take care of my security commitments.

This morning on the way home teams of black youths, working in twos and threes, used the buses to get to staging points. They were not headed to school, but rather hitched their bikes to the rack on the front of the bus and fanned out into the residential areas. There were two teams of two on my bus, listening to hard core rap, cranked up to see if the driver would challenge them. She normally does, but did not today. Two of them followed me for a mile and a half through side streets. I eventually stepped out in front of them hoping to dump one and they took evasive action and sped off; not joking, posturing, threatening or engaging in any of the juvenile simian antics they would normally. They seemed to be on a mission and evaded me as soon as I proved a retaliatory target.

A coworker whose mother dates a cop said that military contractors—including snipers—have been brought in to protect the two stadiums.

A National Guard member told me that the hood rats are avoiding them like the plague and either ignoring or trying to get at the police, of whom they appear to have no fear.

Police sirens are already 4 in Hamilton this morning, where we normally only have 2 per week in the morning. This is a an inversion of the pre-riot pattern of having police sirens wailing through the night, silent in the morning, and sporadic in the afternoon. We now have near-silence in the afternoon, total silence at night, and moderate activity in the morning.

Baltimore, I think, has changed, for the interesting.

Breaking Crystal
A Young White Woman Stranded Among the Hoodrat Hordes

There was zero police coverage in Western Baltimore County, the toughest precinct with the most aggressive cops, who have reduced crime by 11% over the past year. During the day the coverage is half normal. At night, they are all protecting the white people who matter, not the working whites of Middle River, who have their own population of urban blacks. The blacks of Hawthorne have migrated out of the worst neighborhood in East Baltimore, where projects were leveled a few years ago, to set up their drug dealing and pimping businesses among the stoners of this waterfront community.

They are notably absent from our store. Before the riots, we had thugs in there flexing and posturing at us. Since the riots, and the disappearance of the police, they have not ventured onto the lot. The neighborhood blacks have had numerous fights with us on the store front and have not fared well. It occurs to me that we are now the militia strongpoint, the only body of cohesive, able-bodied men in this area. Miss Mary's son, who once lost his job here beating the shit out of four armed hoodrats on the front walk—and throwing one through the window—stops in to check on us. He's a prime athlete with a kind demeanor and about 20 knife scars from attacks by his fellow blacks.

At 2:55, as I finish my break, a middle-aged black man brings a fat, well-dressed, young white girl through the front door and gives her to Bubba, who has me summon our night captain. She is crying her eyes out.

She is pretty, about 5' 8" and 230 pounds, with red hair in pig tails, a tastefully chosen outfit suitable for upscale dining, and thankfully functional footwear, consisting of some kind of sandals. Her powdery makeup is caked and she is heaving her chest, about to pass out.

Crystal had gone out to dance with a friend, who dropped her off at her grandparent's house instead of in the city where the curfew is in force. Her grandparents were either dead asleep or absent. She ran her phone dead calling them as she stood out front.

After about a half hour a group of black men spotted her and approached.

She walked off toward the shopping center.

They followed her.

She picked up her pace.

They picked up their pace.

She began to run.

They began to run after her, and she panicked, screaming and running faster than she had ever thought possible.

One of our customers—a mature black man with a big round head and thick nose tackle build—spotted the savage pursuit, pulled over, got her in the car, and made his way to our location.

The thugs did not pursue.

We have a box of pallet slats for defending the store and our night captain has a reputation for chasing punks through the neighborhood.

As he took care of her and helped her make calls— allowing her to use the office as a safe room—I went back to work.

This morning at six, when Bubba was getting off, I asked him, "What happened with Crystal?"

He frowned and drawled, "She could not get in touch with anyone and we're not allowed to leave the store and go back in the neighborhood. I called the cops at 3:19 and they did not even answer. I called them again at 3:45 and they said they were dispatching an officer. He never came."

I said, "Yeah, because he's over in Towson protecting the white bread."

He then shrugged his shoulders and said, "She walked off, hopefully down Eastern and not back into the neighborhood."

When Big Chev, our virulent hard case racist customer, came down the aisle, I told him about

Crystal and the black guy that saved her, and he responded, "With the cops all mamma's boys and pussies, and letting these monkeys do what they want, this is what you get. When the good coons like him are gone, what will the world be like then? It'll be Planet of the Apes—and it will be what we deserve for not slaughtering these animals."

Miss Ezz's Eye Candy Armageddon

A Prop For You Soldiers Who Thought You Weren't Appreciated

"What beautiful weather. If I was Chinese I'd write a poem. Ah, fuck it."

Mescaline Franklin, 4/29/15

After all of the liberal spin extolling the innocence of the black youth army that defeated the BPD on Monday, it was nice to speak with some real people with real opinions who were at ground level. As much as I write about social emasculation, it was refreshing to speak with a woman who is a man fan, who was there through it all.

I finally got back in touch with Miss Ezz, the lady that notified the BPD that the hood rat brigades would be attacking on Monday. Or rather she got in touch with me while she was smoking on her lunch break.

"How are you doing over there in the war zone, darling?"

"Sugar, this girl is groovin' with this eye candy! I ought to write that stupid bitch that runs the city a thank you letter. You know how long it's been since I've seen more than two good looking muscle men at a time—and white at that! I'm standing here in a high and tight uniformed hunk paradise."

"Are you talking about the national guard?"

"Talking, talking? You know better than that, Baby Cakes. This girl is checking out the merchandise. The boss might be getting bled dry, but I haven't been panhandled, back-sassed, or yelled at since these boys rolled up. Umm, umm, umm, muscles, uniforms, guns—and they're packin'! A hundred handsome white men; I'll stand next to this fellow all day long—got to go sweetie."

'Rock, Paper, Scissors'
Columbine Joe! #1

Last night I was walking through a posh upscale development that used to be a subsidized ghetto called The Village of Tall Trees; a ramshackle maze of wood-panel apartments, inhabited primarily by drug users and the black drug gangs that distributed city heroin and crack into Eastern Baltimore County through this hub.

In 1994 I saw a white man on his knees in the street as I cruised by on the #23 bus as three black men beat him with bats. A cop was also cruising by as the man was beaten down. Now the cop car was on the other side of the bus and could not see the head being smashed in the street, so we really can't fault the cop. I was once nearly alone on this bus with a young woman, at about 7 p.m., when it was fired on and hit with a handgun that I did not see.

Last night, as I walked through this area, I walked with a man in his late 30s who would have been a teen back then. I soon discovered, by the time we were speaking at my job site, that he was a customer, and had been one of the white stoners that lived there with the blacks back in the day.

Columbine Joe

We are franchising out—New York and Boston imitating our violent citizens. It makes me feel alive, reminds me of the old days when I was a young dude living in Tall Trees. I wouldn't want to live like that now. The stress would kill me. But I also would not take back the past. Those stories I collected to tell my children well illustrate why they need to listen up and not live like I did.

They called me Columbine Joe because I wore a trench coat, had long hair and piercings. I probably would have been dead without the Trench Coat Mafia mystique. It freaked the black dudes out. I had this one neighbor who was really cool—didn't talk to him for a year. Then one day we have a conversation, and he tells me about how they all associated me and my roommate with that tragedy out in Colorado. There *was* a lot more to surviving in Tall Trees than that.

My roommate and I were the only ones who worked in the community. I've been held up, shot at, and have seen two murders. Right off the bat we have three black dudes kick in the front door and one of them has a shotgun. They have the drop on us. We have knives and a thirty-eight special but were looking down the barrel of a shotgun. They're taking our stuff: a VCR—which tells you how long ago it was—play station, some other stuff, and they want the CDs. The guy with the gun tells me to put all of my CDs in a bag.

That was just too much. I said, "Look brother, you have the shotgun, you have the power, so you take what you want. But the hell if I'm going to help you rob me and be an accomplice in my own robbery. Take what you're going to take and walk on."

And they don't take all the CDs! How lazy can you be! After they leave, I said to my roommate, "That's a black powder shotgun. You know what that means—short range and one shot."

My roommate grabs his thirty-eight and pops off some rounds at them while they are crossing the street, and they drop some of our stuff, so it wasn't a total loss.

So now we are no longer a door kicking mark because they know about the gun. We hear from some others that they plan on breaking in while we are at work and taking my computer, which is worth like eighteen-hundred dollars. We had to think of something. They would all hang around outside in the common area—all the drug dealers, just like in The Wire. That and Homicide were the two most accurate crime shows ever, better than documentaries.

We go down to the butcher shop on Mace Avenue and ask the owner for a raw beef heart. He thinks were nuts, but he gives us one. We knew this was a dicey proposition. But when you're dealing with these people, you need an image they are going to respect. You also need to be cool, but that's another story.

They pack guns. We primarily had blades. We knew that the guy that did this was in danger of just getting popped, so we drew 'rock, paper, scissors'. As luck would have it I lost. I got all bloody, grabbed the heart in my left hand, grabbed a blade in my right and charged outside into the common area screaming, "Why'd you make me do it, Joe, why? Why?!"

They fucking boogied!

And they called the cops! Can you believe that shit, drug dealers calling the cops?

An hour later—which back then was a good response time—a cop knocks on the door. Of course we're assholes for even living there. He says, "Look I don't even believe the story I've been told. What's going on?"

We let him inside and told him the whole plan. He said, "You guys are freagin' brilliant! I can help you out."

So he just walks out and tells them that he wasn't going to pursue the complaint, because he couldn't find the murder weapon. After that, I'm fuckin' Columbine. As long as I'm cool and don't engage in any bullshit or snitchin' I'm okay.

Those were the days man—would not trade those experience for the world. Like the guy that wrote Angela's ashes said, "A painless childhood is worthless," or something to that effect. From fifteen to twenty-four, I lived a lifetime and I'll tell you all about it.

A Baltimorean Asks

I am concerned that there will be more trouble on Friday. I believe the autopsy report will be released on Friday.

Betty

Whatever you have planned for Friday in Baltimore get it done before 11:00. The hood rats don't slink furtively from their trash strewn dens until 11:00 a.m. or 1:00 p.m. Morning traffic today was at 5% of normal in the city.

The younger gang members and leaders have been scouting in the mornings. But the assault units won't be out until after lunch.

And Betty, the police are unable to protect themselves and have been directed to let citizens fend for themselves. The only safe place is beyond bus lines, about 10 miles north, west and east of the city. If you get in trouble, the National Guard have demonstrated the ability to hold and take open ground, unlike the cops. Getting close to cops will just put you in danger. If you see a cop, pretend you are in a horror movie and some idiot just went down the hall to check on the creaking door, and stay put or go the other way.

Be careful of outlying areas where blacks live. The county hood rats have began to notice that all of the police are in Towson protecting the rich. The crime is popping up in the county, not being responded to by the police and not being reported by the media priesthood.

Take care.

Charles M   April 30, 2015 7:18 PM EDT

You're making it sound like we're in a permanent Rut.

Or maybe I'm thinking it.

JL   **responds:** April 30, 2015 10:18 PM EDT

More like a trash chute.

'Does the Curfew Make You Angry?'

'How Does It Make You Feel To Be Told You Have to Be Inside By Ten?'

"I know you're loving this. But I also know how deep your defiant streak is. Be careful and keep your head on a swivel."

Ajay

Managing the Slave Master

I'm not some kind of Libertarian that believes in rights, or a liberal or conservative government slave that believes in doing what he is told by his master. My fractional autonomy strategy is to coexist with the massive festering puss bag of civilization where honor has no place, in such a way as to preserve my senses of self, spirit and honor.

Just like the criminals who are still quietly looting Baltimore and pouncing on the unaware, I have gamed the system. In fact, the entire neighborhood is doing it—the main drag a party until 9:30—with people walking around drinking in violation of container laws, knowing that the pigs—if they show up—will not do so until 10 and will stick to the primary roads as the party spreads down side streets. Tonight was a festive occasion with a huge number of white people on the street enjoying some freedom from the everyday tyranny of black muggers, who are busy looting stores and messing with the Pixie Dust Police Department.

Yes, the curfew is unjust and rankles a bit and is also ineffective, already being gamed to criminal advantage. I will find my freedom in bits and pieces somewhere, and most importantly between my ears.

If you are interested in my specific strategies and tactics, read **Taboo You**, my handbook for being a subversively defiant asshole.

How Can the Police Be Strengthened?
A Baltimorean Asks the Wrong Person

Overall I think the riots are great, as the Kentucky Fried Mayor's national broadcast that the looters had to be permitted to destroy what they wished, as well as the open admission of the police force that they would only protect certain positions and themselves and had no ability to protect citizens, will hopefully be remembered by all, as we enter the rocky plateau of our end time and lurch from riot to riot. We are going the way of Rome, and I say bring on the dark ages. Remember, that for most of those you know, these events will be erased by the media priests through their portals of indoctrination before the year is out.

The Baltimore City Police Department cannot be properly funded on the narrow tax base available. There are more criminals than home owners in Harm City. The BPD is kept on life support by Federal money, which is tied to drug war stipulations. The BPD is therefore structured as a law enforcement strike force, not a public defense force. The BPD specializes in strikes against individuals. Almost all BPD actions are essentially heavily armed gang attacks on individuals or a house.

From my experience and police and criminal interviews, the operational doctrine is roughly this:

1 unarmed, unaggressive, and perhaps uncooperative shoplifter, requires 2 police officers and a store security person to process, whereas the store security person probably handled the person on their own. The BPD dilemma is that their officers are armed with firearms. They cannot take a chance of an officer being defeated in a one-to-one struggle and having their weapon taken by a violent criminal.

1 unarmed, aggressive shoplifter requires 3 to 7 police officers. I saw this at an Aldi's store last year.

1 suspected criminal, assumed to be armed, in his house, which is assumed to be a drug stash house, will require a full tactical squad or more.

Above we see the BPD trained, organized, and operating in 2-1 to 10-1 attacks against various types of individuals.

In military terms 3-1 odds is considered a bare minimum for any commander considering an attack. 1-1 is regarded as suicide. The Russians considered 7-1 odds mandatory for hitting a German position in WWII. 7-1 odds is the base advantage you want against fortified positions— which would be the drug stash house. Out in the open 7-1 is slaughter—that would be George Armstrong Custer and his 7th Cavalry—or perhaps Freddie-G against the bicycle cops and patrolmen.

With any force of this type that is organized along such predatory lines, defending against equal odds becomes a huge, hard to adapt to, headache. Defending against superior force is likely to be a disaster—primarily a crisis of morale—or fighting spirit. Metaphorically speaking an urban police force is a bully, whose members are trained to operate from a position of overwhelming advantage in terms of numbers, tactical surprise and equipment.

What typically happens to a bully when someone stands up to him? When someone attacks him? When someone gangs up on him?

Once conditioned to bully, the habit may come ingrained in the individual. Six years ago, a black police officer demanded that I open the store for him after hours. When I refused from behind the glass he fingered his badge and promised to beat my ass on the street the next time he saw me. My co-manager once had three cops try to bully him into cashing a third party check. After he refused, they stalked him after work. I am not making these points to excuse citizen hatred for cops but to demonstrate that the very mode of operation for urban law officers is often corrosive to the masculine spirit—which is to say the warrior spirit, which is what you need to deal with an aggressive mob.

I do not blame the officers, as much as I dislike the way they have treated me as an individual. The vast majority of them treated me well as a store manager, saving my ass on a few occasions. I blame their handlers, the system that tries to make of them attack dogs in a doomed drug war and then betrays them in their extremity.

The only way I see to strengthen a police department so that it can protect its own and the noncriminal population, is to end the drug war, which has them splitting their time between protecting and attacking drug gangs, which just generates a tougher class of criminal to prey upon the population.

Honky Cracker   May 3, 2015 4:10 PM EDT

But to demonstrate that the very mode of operation for urban law officers is often corrosive to the masculine spirit-which is to say the warrior spirit, which is what you need to deal with an aggressive mob.

I read this so many times that I lost count! This statement had to be divinely inspired by a God of War, a masculine God or Lafond has hit a level of a Warrior that is unbelievable for a civilian.

I'm going to pay him for letting me write this.

 **responds:** May 8, 2015 6:04 PM EDT

Thanks a lot for the prop Honky Cracker!

I remember a magazine from the 1970s titled Warriors, which was written for martial artist, fighters, military and law enforcement. I doubt if they could even sell that thing these days. This feminine governance style has to drive a cop crazy, if he was one of those cops that was choosing either military or law enforcement so it was a way to remain masculine. As much as I have animosity to cops, I want masculine cops, not some sissy telling me what to do!

I must go. The God of War is channeling through me—and he wants beer!

'America's Microcosm'
A Zero Hedge Post that Nails the Baltimore Riots

The quote at the head of this article is from the author of The Wire, who was a Baltimore reporter during the worst times, when this hunting template of police work was honed to a rarified form.

I like the slant on this article. I would just like to add that the collective mind of Baltimore is so twisted from abuse that what is left is utterly beyond reform or redemption. I'm still smugly proud to have survived 30 years on the low end of this crime vector.

http://www.zerohedge.com/news/2015-04-30/baltimore-microcosm-america

War Drums

In this article David Simon lays out not only the history of the BPD dysfunctionality, but the root cause of it's problem, as well. With Mr. Simon going on the record to lengths that "The Wire" never did (despite the fact it was quite the complex and nuanced show), how can Martin O'Malley remain a candidate for president? Simon has laid out one of the most powerful cases against MO'M. How his opponents wouldn't use it is beyond me. Simon saw his city burning and must have said "enough is enough" and aimed his pen directly at the heart of the 'Teflon Leprechaun.'

responds: May 1, 2015 5:55 PM EDT

In 'The Wire,' all you have to see is the few meetings about drug arrest stats and the massaging of the numbers, and a little imagination, to imagine the process ending up right here. It is amazing to me that so many folks have seen that entre series—and Homicide—and still choose to believe that the 'protect and serve' motto on the police cruisers means anything other than 'protecting political office holders and serving the crime stat juker.'

'Not Here!'
A Bright Spot in the Dark Baltimore Story

Last night I was at a bar watching CNN and Fox News. These channels reflected the two dueling templates for American thought, both of which walk in the dream space of delusion.

On the Left, is only concern over the death of a drug dealer, with no concern for the death of hundreds of others killed within the last year. White women hunted in the streets of Baltimore by black men and being rescued by yet other black men, does not even a story make. The only story is the feminist urge to leftist conformity.

On the Right, it might as well be the Israelis against the Arabs, and we know who our friends are. The underlying belief on the Right is that all urban blacks are mindless animals who attack on sight and cannot be reasoned with or coexisted with. Ironically, the leftward drive to keep the races and genders at each other's throats feeds the rightward drive for separatism, making American media and politics a symbiotic union for the generation of social despair.

Few people see this, and the media wishes to do nothing to disabuse us of the notion that black people have any agency. Both the liberal Democratic Left and the conservative Republican Right agree absolutely on one thing, that blacks have no agency, and that they are dysfunctional children of the nation who must have decisions made for them. The only disagreement is on the course of action. The Left wants to be mommy doling out hugs and rewards, and the Right wants to be daddy, slapping that behind.

The one thing we can't have is an example of blacks working on their own to assert their Will, their agency, their morality, their spirit.

1. On Wednesday night, when a black man brought a white woman to our job site who had been being pursued by a gang of black men, this was an example of agency that cannot be let free in the media by either the Right or Left.

2. On Monday night, when Boomy, a black man, saved a 'blonde woman of the yuppies' from two armed gangs of rampaging black men, he was showing a kind of heroism that used to make a story—but must now be swept under the rug. The news cameras have not strayed from the central narrative. No news truck has penetrated the real Baltimore where people live and must now police themselves, as the police protect the narrative and leadership of both sides.

3. Likewise, on Monday, when the privately owned Shoprite supermarket, just up the road from the scene of the main battle, where Mondawmin Mall suffered over a million in damage, came under attack while the police were defending their corporate Minnesota-based competitor down the street, what happened? The black customers from the neighborhood formed a human wall and said, "No, not here, not to our market, you don't."

That story of black human agency must be denied by the Left and the Right, both consisting of rich whites and their multiracial cronies. The only story CNN wanted to tell was the crusade of our black female prosecutor to convict the cops who killed G-man. If it is not gender against gender, race against race, there is no story. And the story least likely to be told, as with the three above, will be the tale that will point out that black Americans make individual, moral decisions and take consequent mortal risks every day, in simple pursuit of truth and liberty, and these two concepts have no place in the narrative.

When two parents fight over a troubled child—as the political Left and Right in this nation seem to be doing with the black community—the last thing they are willing to consider is that that child might have a will of his own and more importantly, that he might have more sense than either one of his dysfunctional parents.

jr May 1, 2015 2:36 PM EDT

Regarding media reporting, did you see this news story regarding the mother of six walloping her 16-year-old son in front of the TV cameras: http://www.cbsnews.com/news/baltimore-mother-toya-graham-on-why-she-smacked-son-i-dont-want-him-to-be-a-freddie-gray/

She saw him in a black hoodie about to engage in some extra-curricular activity, which she dealt with quite brusquely and physically. Her being more powerfully built and tougher apparently than her son, he didn't have a chance.

Everybody loved the story. She became a heroine of the Left and Right. The Left because it fits the Narrative of the strong single mother. The Right, I guess, because they love tough love.

Thinking back on your previous articles regarding the somewhat toxic relationship between some mothers and their sons, I think they got it all wrong.

I got wind of this on a manosphere site, where the take home point was if it was a man/father doing the walloping he would have been arrested. (https://dalrock.wordpress.com/2015/04/29/black-fathers-dont-matter/). I'm pretty sure that misses the point too.

I was just wondering what your point of view is on it.

responds: May 1, 2015 5:30 PM EDT

Of course it depends on the two of them and their relationship. My guess is she is not the abusive type. The really abusive types don't care where their kid is and tend to beat him at home when he's this old, often with a weapon and closed fist. My hunch is she was being the best father she knows how to be.

The Harm City Lesson
Urban and Suburban Collapse Notes

As I write on Friday 1:30 p.m., my contact at
Mondawmin informs me that squads of 10-15
students were breaking out of school and headed to
the plundered mall as an 'armored column' of the
National Guard rolled up to meet them in five Hum-
vees and a large armored vehicle.

Now that the charges have been announced for the
police whose everyday conduct finally brought on a
riot they could not handle, I think we are out of the
woods until the next media frenzy, or something
really serious, like an interruption of EBT cash and
food stamp distributions, which causes another
riot.

173

What did I observe on the ground that can be broken into operational elements for the next Harm City riot?

1. The only effective police units are the tactical squads with armored vehicles, with the police sedan being a virtual deathtrap in an urban environment.

2. Only key political and corporate positions were protected.

3. The police announced that they had no ability or intention to protect anyone but themselves and the political elite. Even the press was told to fend for themselves.

4. The entire residential breadth of the city was abandoned to criminals with zero police presence during riot activity.

5. Most business sectors were abandoned to the criminals, with zero police presence.

6. Upscale urban enclaves were not protected! In the city, only political and major corporate entities benefited from police protection.

7. In outlying suburban areas, all available police were directed to choke points where the city mobs could get to the upper class York Road corridor north of Towson. All middle-class, working class, and poor Baltimore County districts were completely stripped of police manpower for the night time hours and run on half strength during the day. There was no increase in daytime crime, but an increase in crime at night, which makes sense as most police engage in harassment work rather than deterrence.

8. It took more than 24 hours before any cohesive plan was initiated to take back control of the city, with crime in outlying areas continuing to be high for the duration of the week.

9. Peaceful protests had as much of a negative effect on outlying areas as violent protests, as the police were diverted for each.

Assessing the Combatants

I will use the Operational Combat Series action rating scale to grade the effectiveness of both sides. The scale is as follows.

5 = elite

4 = veteran

3 = operational standard

2 = below standard

1 = poor

0 = ineffective

The way this system of unit action rating works is on a comparative basis with a difference of 2 imparting an overwhelming operational advantage.

Criminal Units

Overall, in terms of strategic and tactical execution, the criminal syndicates that stage-managed the riots and the corollary looting rated:

-High school kids tasked with confronting the police as a rock-armed mob= 2

-Gang members tasked with terrorizing outlying areas, armed with bats in groups of 5-15 = 3

-Break-in teams, who raided over 100 businesses in Northeast and East Baltimore without arrests, or casualties = 4

Defense Forces

-Patrol officers in sedans were completely ineffective, sustained casualties, and lost equipment = 0

-Police organized in riot gear managed to hold their ground but demonstrated poor tactical mobility, sustained casualties, and lost equipment = 1 or 2

-Police tactical squads were effective but under utilized by their commanders = 3

-National Guard units = 4

-Gun-armed home owners stopped two patrols of gang members in Gardenville, and two male motorists rescued women targeted for gang rape on the East Side, demonstrating a level of effectiveness on par with the Guard units = 4

The criminal success was largely due to avoiding guard contact and evading tactical squads while targeting the static units, patrol officers and civilian population. Seeing as the forces were evenly matched in quality, I credit the anonymous gang leadership with superior planning and decision making, and the political and police leadership with gross neglect.

Below is an index of articles related to the subject of urban collapse and mob violence:

The Fall Of The Garden Of Ishtar

On The Coming Riots

A Night Of Cozy Unrest In Harm City

Rise Of The Nike Nation

Getting Hammered In The Hood

Travolta   May 1, 2015 9:02 PM EDT

We recently discovered that Baltimore's school system is in debt up to at least 60 million dollars, with rumors that it could be as high as 100 million.

Contrast that with Chicago who has a school system

in debt to the tune of 1.1 BILLION dollars. The Illinois state government has made it clear that it will not bail out the school system, mostly due to the fact that the state is running a deficit of 5.5 billion. Chicago's debt rating was recently downgraded to one step above junk. Chicago's primary source of funding, outside of municipal bonds, is the real estate tax. To begin to even meet its bond payments the city will have to double those taxes overnight. I give Chicago two years, at best, before it too defaults. When it defaults, expect all city contracts to be renegotiated, including pay, health and retirement benefits for all employees.

"The city failed to cut its recurring expenditures to match its recurring revenues after it blew through its reserve funds. Instead, two administrations have:

> Used long-term debt to finance everyday expenses and maintenance;

> Used long-term debt to finance judgments and settlements, including police brutality cases, and retroactive wage increases and pension contributions for its unionized employees;

> Restructured the city's existing debt to extend the maturities on its bonds far out into the future in order to avoid having to pay the debt as it was coming due;

> Borrowed more money than it needed in order to make payments on the bonds it was issuing to avoid debt service expenses, essentially using debt to pay debt; and

> Possibly used the city's portfolio of interest rate derivatives as an ATM.

State and local governments typically issue bonds to finance the construction of buildings and infrastructure that will benefit residents for generations..."

http://finance.yahoo.com/news/how-chicago-has-used-financial-engineering-to-paper-over-its-massive-budget-gap-144515066.html

"A post-election property tax increase is inevitable to solve Chicago's $20 billion pension crisis, one of Mayor Rahm Emanuel's most powerful City Council allies warned Monday, arguing that anybody who claims otherwise is living in a dream world.

Nine aldermen allied with Emanuel joined his campaign co-chair, City Clerk Susana Mendoza, at a City Hall news conference to put the heat on mayoral challenger Jesus "Chuy Garcia" for making $1.9 billion in promises that, they claim, would force the owner of a $250,000 home to pay $1,900 more in annual property taxes..."

http://chicago.suntimes.com/chicago-politics/7/71/425927/emanuel-ally-warns-post-election-property-tax-hike

Travolta   May 1, 2015 4:39 PM EDT

Chicago will be next, bank on it. Given Chi-town's reputation I doubt their city police will be as incompetent or restrained.

If there's something that could once again set off protests/riots in B'more, it would be acquittal of all the officers charged, IMO. It will be interesting to see how long it take to go to trial.

responds: May 1, 2015 5:34 PM EDT

It will be interesting to see where the trial is held.

Chicago actually has a tax base to support a pretty autonomous police force so I imagine those cops will fare better than these. The BPD has essentially become an outpost for the federal drug war. I don't even regard it as much of a police force, but rather as a support system for combating the home grown drug gangs.

The Arsenal At Your Feet
Mescaline Franklin Steps Into The Man Cave to Acquire Skull Crushing Wisdom For the Coming Stone Age

"Was the stone the first weapon, the thing that evolved into the club, and into the bats that these savages are smashing in car windows with? Or was it the stick? Which one do you think came first—and of course, why?"

We are going back millions of years with this question to the time when small hominids—like the size of an elementary school child—were skulking around lion and hyena kills. They probably placed above the jackals right off the bat, and were able to run off Cheetahs. They were hunted by leopards and were most likely competing head to head with the African dog packs.

Essentially, the behavior downtown this week was more similar to kill scavenging than to war or hunting. Early man was no hunter.

The first weapon could have been a stick if the right piece of branchless, desiccated wood happened to be lying around. Stick weapons are generally impractical until you have stone tools to shape them.

Obviously, while scavenging the bottom end of a kill—particularly a cheetah or leopard kill—these fellows would have wanted the bone marrow. The easiest way to get at it is to crack open a long bone. This would be best done over a stone at first, and then with a smaller handier stone that could be carried. I imagine the use of the ungulate femur bone as a club coming into fashion at virtually the same time as the handheld stone during the course of scavenging.

For instance, let's suppose, at a primordial Mondawmin Mall, Tyrone Erectus was about to smash open the femur of a zebra with a stone, and Terrence Erectus tried to take it from him? A smash with the stone followed by a finishing blow with the leg bone may well have heralded our ascent to power, every tyrant among us indebted to Tyrone Erectus for his imaginative problem solving skills.

The unaltered stone evolved into the bolo, then the sling stone, and eventually the bullet and cannon ball.

The handheld stone became the hand axe by chipping away at the thing with a hammer stone. This produced flakes that could cut and pierce and therefore gave birth to knives, and projectile heads. Eventually some forms of knives would evolve into a limited selection of small swords. The hand axe evolved into various axes, the apex being the early modern halberd.

The club evolved into the staff weapons, the war club and the oar, which is a handy war club itself. The war club and oar eventually evolved into a wide variety of swords.

The simple stone alone is a formidable weapon, the weapon used to slaughter an entire troop of baboons 700,000 years ago, by David to kill Goliath, and by the students of Frederick Douglas High School to emasculate the Baltimore City Police

Department. As you walk through residential areas on the eve of apocalypse keep an eye out for easily loosened bricks. If attacked, I suggest—if given time—smashing one brick in half on a curb, so that you have two weapons, and because the full size brick can be impractical to throw depending on your physicality. Look at the crumbling ruin of your urban centers and the truck loads of bricks decorating the suburban gardens of the deluded, and you will find an arsenal at your feet.

Oh yes, if you are serious about winning a rock battle. Forget the rocks. Invest in a sack of lacrosse balls, and recruit all of the baseball players you know. Seriously, learn how to throw.

fatmanjudo   May 1, 2015 10:18 PM EDT

I think it was in Paris that they paved over the cobblestones to deprive the people of ammo. Ripping up the streets to throw at cops now that is a serious riot.

You forgot Cain and Able. My vote is for the rock as the first weapon. Good ranged weapon for pests and skull cracker for hand to hand. Plentiful in all seasons and all locations. A group of baseball players could drive off even large predators. Those that can effectively kill at a distance would have a caloric advantage over the hunters who had to get close.

However I do remember reading that Neanderthals did not have the proper shoulder development to throw overhand while Cromags did. If true the Neanderthals would need to use long sticks to gain distance. So the answer may be a biological question concerning the development of movement in the shoulder joint.

'Sorry White People'
Columbine Joe! #2

I have had numerous suburban white women tell me that the female mayor is politically doomed because the black population will be upset with her handling of the riots. Before jumping to such conclusions, we should consider that residents of Baltimore's ghettos are used to a little more excitement than the typical white suburbanite and might even be thankful to the mayor for that closet full of tennis shoes their son hauled home.

You know when you live in a bad area when a car backfires and everyone hits the deck. After living out in Tall Trees for a few months, hitting the floor in a prone position was second nature.

War Drums

Now there was Terrence, who lived downstairs, who used to step outside with his twenty-two pistol every night at nine-forty-five and pop off a few rounds.

One night, I had some straight white friends over from Towson to play Dungeons and Dragons. I was well established in the community as Columbine Joe—people did not fuck with me; crazy white guy with facial piercings, long hair and a trench coat. I'm the guy the cops fuck with first, so there is some value in the community to that as well. Primarily we're living there to be close to the drug supply and be able to smoke when we want. I worked out in Owings Mills—like a two hour commute.

Well, we're sitting there playing D&D, and we hear this pop-pop-pop-pop and my Towson buddies are wigging, "Call the cops, oh my God, call the cops!"

I just said, "Be cool, it's just Terrence. I'll take care of this."

I open the window, and I yell down to Terrence, "Hey Terrence, could you keep it down please. You're scaring my guests. I've got white people from Towson up here."

Terence was cool, yelled back, "Sorry Columbine, Sorry white people. You all have a nice night, white people!"

Terrence was cool like that—good people.

The Wisdom of Swine
Columbine Joe! #3

Now that we are reaping the social unrest awards sown by the drug war, I thought I might provide two brief anecdotes from my new favorite interview to illustrate the high caliber of resource allocation that has attended the waging of this pitiless struggle.

The RV

Okay, we're basically living out in Tall Trees so we can sit on the stoop and smoke dope when we want—don't have to have a city cop clothesline us while we're sitting on our own stoop getting high.

Okay, question is, how many residents of The Village of Tall Trees own a car?

That's right brother—not a one. Now, how many of us own an RV, or know someone who owns an RV?

Heck, if we all pitched in—including the drug dealers—we probably wouldn't have been able to lease one!

So, one day we wake up, go out on the stoop to smoke a bowl, and we're like, hey, an RV, I wonder if that's the FBI or the DEA?

For a month this thing is parked on Dolittle Road, waiting for someone stupid enough to sell drugs right in front of it. We started yelling at them, "Hello, FBI, we are not going to buy drugs in front of your RV. Perhaps you can better spend the tax payers' money elsewhere?"

We used to play around daring people to go knock on the door and wondering if anyone would be stupid enough to do a buy in front of them.

Well, one day it was gone, not a bust. The thing sat there for a month. That had to cost a couple of bucks.

The Cardboard City Crew

That, of course, is only one of many examples of law enforcement incompetence when it came to dealing with us. There was this period of time when we all hung out down in Cardboard City [a homeless camp in a roadside wood].

To be clear, we did not deal drugs. We certainly did our share of drugs. We bought drugs. We shared drugs; perhaps even derived a mutual benefit from our association. That was, after all, the entire point of the thing. One thing we were not, was organized.

My best bud was Jerry, a real cool dude, nice guy— but not too smart. You give Jerry two choices and he always takes the wrong one. His low IQ trait was pronounced enough that he essentially knew it. At least he was not guilty of the sin of being stupid and thinking he was brilliant.

Well, he's not there one day. I'm sitting there dropping acid and the cops roll up. I'm like, *Oh my God, I'm in trouble. I hope they don't know about the acid.*

But not to worry. The cops, they wanted Jerry. They said, "We know you're a member of the Cardboard City Crew."

I'm like, "What? You mean you gave us a name?"

"Yes," they insist, "the Cardboard City Crew is an established drug ring, an ongoing criminal enterprise."

My head was spinning. I was dumfounded in one sense, but in another I was relieved, and felt quite confident that they had nothing on me that would stick. I was like, "Look, do you see us, do you see where we hang out. Don't you think if we were an actual drug gang we would have our shit together just a little bit?"

The one cop says, "What about Jerry, your leader. We heard you were close to him."

First of all, I burst into uncontrollable laugher. Nobody that knew Jerry would think he was a leader. I said, "Of course I'm close to him. He's my best friend. We hang out together. And as much as I love Jerry, if we were all in a burning building and it was up to Jerry to lead us out, we'd be toast!"

I leveled with the cops and said, "Look, I don't know who sold you all on this tip about our supposed 'gang' but they sold you some bad information."

I told Jerry later on and he was like, "Me, really, a king pin? Good to know!"

Dude I could talk about misinformed cops all night long. I suppose for them it was all a grope in the dark.

To Neglect the Dead
Columbine Joe #4

The Village of Tall Trees was one of those Baltimore satellite ghettos, a slice of city misery sunk into the county landscape, thanks to subsidized housing vouchers and bus lines curiously routed from the worst ghetto in West Baltimore to its annex in East Baltimore County. The Village was served by the #23, which no longer turns around up at the 7-11, because the village is no longer there but has been replaced by an upscale housing development, complete with duck pond and flag. One cringes when considering what the occupants of Tall Trees would have used the duck pond for. With Baltimore City cops now infamous for brutality, and being blamed with causing the low income residents to be brutal as well, it is easy to forget that brutality is a two way street and that the cops might just be catching the inhumanity bug from those they police.

On the Stoop with Leroy

I'm sitting out on my stoop one night. It's nice and dark. I'm smoking a bowl and Leroy—two stoops down—a black crack head—is doing what he does.

Then Leroy's dealer shows up, walks up to Leroy with three of his associates. They speak a few words, none of which I can—or care to—hear, and then "blam-blam-blam!"

Somehow I kept my cool. It was at least a thirty-eight. I could not see it, only the muzzle flash. I couldn't tell you if it was an automatic or a revolver. It definitely was not a twenty-two or twenty-five.

You know, I'm Columbine right, they expect me to be cool. So I just give him the hand signal, nod that we're cool, and turn around, and go inside, and they're on their way.

They knew I did not snitch and never came after me. I can't believe how many people said I should have called the cops, testified even. They knew I knew, saw that I saw. I was in no hurry to join Leroy.

The Dumpster

My roommate and I worked out in Owings Mills—a two hour commute. We are dropping off the trash on the way to the bus stop. I open the dumpster to throw my trash in, and there is a body.

He was a black man. There really is no other answer to that question—it's always a black body, and of course, always a black person that put it there. When I think back I can't believe how calm I was.

This was before cell phones—or before many people had them. So I walk over to the pay phone, call nine-one-one, and tell them, "Hey I'm at the village of Tall Trees over on Dolittle Road, and there is a body in the dumpster."

And it gets ridiculous, immediately. The operator wants to know what the corpse is wearing, how old it was, do I know his name, what is my name, why am I here, etc.

I'm like, "Look. None of that matters. Who I am does not matter. What matters is you have a body in the dumpster. Now I'm going to work. Thank you, and goodbye!"

I work eight hours, come home from work—so this is a twelve hour span, and I have to check. So I go over to the dumpster, open it, and there it is, the body in the dumpster. I definitely felt like I had to do something or this poor guy was going to end up in a landfill.

I went over to the pay phone, called nine-one-one, and they repeat all the same bullshit, who am I, where do I live, why am I there. Eventually I just say, "Look, this has gotten to the point where you are losing evidence. This body has been in the dumpster for at least twelve-fourteen hours—you need to come get this man, okay!"

They came and got the body but took their time doing it. It makes you wonder, in this day and age, with no pay phones, do you call on your cell phone?

I mean, I was obviously a suspect just for phoning it in. How many people just keep walking by so that they don't have to become a suspect? How many bodies have made it to the landfill?

60,000 Dope Fiends and Counting
News Max Gives a Rundown of G-man Riot News Caught in the Media Filter and Still Doesn't Scratch the Surface

This is a pretty on point rundown of 17 overlooked items. Interestingly enough, even these 17 items, overlooked by the mainstream press, barely expands the story beyond the death of one man in police custody and the riots centered around the Mondawmin area and the Courthouse and Stadium.

There has been an effective news blackout of this event. When the police take an area off of their patrol or response radar, so does the press. If you want to get a small taste of what the media/government does not want you to know what went on in Baltimore since last Friday check the other articles under our 2015 Baltimore Travel Guide tag. These are simply the experiences of a few handfuls of Baltimore area residents, just a tiny slice of what really went on.

The most fascinating thing about this spate of urban unrest, is that it is going undocumented as the entire nation stares witlessly at the mayor, the prosecutor, and the decoy brigade of rioters who are running interference for the army of professional criminals looting the sectors of the city where no reporter or cop dare tread and where no politician cares to visit. It is shocking, even to me, how easy it has been for the media to convince America that a city has not been looted but just one black neighborhood. An aggressive social narrative is such a powerful thing in the hands of our media that even the opposition and nonbelievers buy the lie by default.

I hope this hasty body of work, compiled over the course of the week, at least puts an apostrophe on the lie that is the accepted story.

http://www.newsmax.com/newswidget/17-things-baltimore-riots/2015/04/30/id/641793/?Dkt_nbr=13E09-

1&nmx_source=Inquisitr&nmx_medium=widget&n mx_content=454&nmx_campaign=widgetphase2

Jim Fry   May 2, 2015 12:19 AM EDT

Yes, we reap the sown propaganda, over, and over, and ...

I am curious on just one point and would appreciate your perspective:

"17. Just 25 percent of U.S. adults consider the riots to be an expression of legitimate outrage, according to a new Rasmussen Report survey, which said 63 percent characterize it as mostly criminals taking advantage of the situation."

Isn't this exactly what the most organized gang, our politicians, do daily, as they take advantage of the situation, seeking to manage the collective paradigm? I'm not excusing violence by any individual or side, merely reflecting on what appear to be facts, which are, that the employed strategies, which both sides, appear to leverage, appear identical and the concomitant consequences are most similar.

'Man Down'
Street Level Riot Videos From Baltimore

If you have ever wondered what 'untrained' means in a contact situation, that is the definition of the first video. Some of the police are unfit, some female, and most of them are having trouble seeing with the head gear on, causing them to lift their chins and expose themselves to the type of damaging blow taken by the casualty. This engagement is a classic rout of a superior heavy force by a mobile light force. These cops have not been trained to work as a unit larger than two, and many of them seem unable to stay in the front rank out of sheer timidity. I could only imagine what a Roman Centurian would have done to these slackers.

The second is a mix of cell phone video, that ends with a snap shot of the proud toilet paper looter. His photo occupies the entire second half of the video.

https://www.youtube.com/watch?v=qFzjkNkVcPU

https://www.youtube.com/watch?v=84s-s_hXuhk

SMART ASS WHITE BOY   May 3, 2015 10:20 AM EDT

The thin blue line has collapsed and a song keeps playing in my head "It's the end of the world as we know it and I feel fine". Stay safe my friend.

responds: May 8, 2015 6:18 PM EDT

You know, that's a real smart ass thing to say white boy.

Thanks, will do.

Reign of Fear
The Unreported Race Purge in Baltimore County

I spent my time out and about today, inquiring into the events in the lives of people I do not normally have contact with. These are all residents of Eastern Baltimore County, the precinct that was stripped bare of police officers to provide protection for the County Seat of Towson.

Jerry, an emergency room physician, treated 14 lacerations and broken bones above his normal workload, all of which were the result of unreported black on white attacks.

As with the city, stats on violent crimes against citizens will seem to dip as no officers are available to document these incidents. Attacks in the County have increased night by night, the criminals knowing that there will be no police response or even a report upon which to base an investigation.

Tuesday night, Marvin was walking to the bus stop when he noticed that black men were giving him hard looks. He noticed, as he neared the stop, that a number of blacks were following him. One picked up a tree limb and hit him in the leg with it from behind, breaking his leg. He was not robbed.

On Wednesday, night Dan was filling up his gas tank at a gas station when a black man rolled onto the parking lot and began blasting the rap lyrics, "Fuck the police." The man was not a customer but was apparently engaging in intimidation. A "red neck," came over to Dan and said, "I'm about sick of this shit. I ought to put some bullet holes in that fucking car."

Dan did not engage in any conversation and got out of there as quietly and quickly as possible.

Also on Tuesday night, Allen was gassing up at a Royal Farms store when he noticed black men, too numerous to count at a glance, gathering around the station and closing in on him. As his car filled up he nonchalantly leaned on the hood of his car with his left hand, drew his handgun with his right, and placed it on the windshield frame above the driver's seat as he whistled. The crowd dispersed immediately.

Billy, a middle-aged man and his elderly mother, live in poverty in the Essex precinct. They have no vehicle and walk to the local Farm Store for their groceries. As they were walking down the street on Thursday night a car load of black men cruised by, screamed that his mother was a "fucking white bitch," and began to throw bottles. One bottle broke on his face, causing a cut. Another bottle bruised and cut his ribs. A rock smashed into and ripped open his upper arm as he shielded his mother. Billy managed to get his mother home after the thugs ran out of ammunition and then made his way to the hospital for treatment.

Across the city and county, whites have declared to me that they are either looking to move away from Baltimore or purchase a firearm. Numerous whites have said they are now afraid to look at blacks and will seek to avoid interracial contact.

In the city, the entitlement pressure continues to ramp up, with the Whole Foods grocery store coming under fire for feeding national guardsmen that prevented their store from being looted. The ghettoites claim that the grocer should have been feeding the black students who lost their free school lunch on Tuesday, rather than the guardsmen who were protecting the grocer from these same juvenile delinquents.

Most working class residents and longtime residents are convinced that these riots were just a taste of things to come.

We will never know how many whites were attacked by blacks, and what kind of attacks they were, because these facts are not in the least important to the NEWS and the Nation. Only dollars lost and police and criminals harmed and arrested are of any interest.

The Hate Train
Was Gentrification A Riot Cause?: Betty Responds to the Apologetic News Spin

"James, I have seen numerous print and broadcast news stories citing urban gentrification as a cause for the riots—one of the underlying reasons for the black on white hate. Are you in the loop on this?"

Betty

Betty, urban gentrification is when the children and grand children of the white people who fled the cities become tired of a continual flight into the countryside that results in a 1-2 hour commute and brings them close to the next urban center. You can only run for so long it seems. There is also the desire to live close to cultural attractions.

Recently the liberal black-identified press has spilled much ink over gentrification taking away black history—such as dice rolling venues behind crumbling buildings and illegal night clubs in the basements of row houses.

The fact of urban gentrification in Baltimore city is that virtually all of the yuppie/hipster urban homesteaders have moved into the traditional working class white enclaves of South Baltimore, Federal Hill, Locust Point [all three of these technically South Baltimore, but settled separately with different displacement patterns], Fells Point, Canton, and Hamden.

For more on this subject read ***White Wednesday Special: Urban Gentrification***

These areas were sought by the first hipster pioneers to benefit from the protection of the tough whites in those areas who had held out against the black on white race purge that was the 70's and 80's in Baltimore. The end result is that the housing values go up so much that the working and poor whites must move out as they can't pay the taxes.

Recently, beginning in the 2000s, Johns Hopkins University and Hospital have been buying up vast swaths of vacant property in East Baltimore [where Boomy the Nigerian cabby rescued the 'blonde woman of the yuppies'] and along the Charles Village Corridor. This was in response to blacks preying on hospital and university staff. These large institutions are buying up the criminal seed beds which constitute perhaps a third of the black Baltimore economy [with welfare constituting roughly another third]. This has caused more damage to the drug gangs than any police action and is covered in the final season of 'The Wire.' Over the past two years a concerted effort to discourage white resettlement of Baltimore has been made by black criminal residents. However, the news spin and statistical manipulation engaged in by the leftist city government has successfully blinded the prospective home buyers to these facts until it is too late.

It is no accident that the prime targets of the mob attacks were the Shoppers supermarket [which was successfully defended thanks to the early warnings put out by black cashiers from the neighborhood] and the CVS drug store, which the Mayor gave orders not to defend. Both of these locations were only established due to city government initiatives to bring businesses into the neighborhood.

Note that the most successful pockets of gentrification, such as South Baltimore, Locust Point and Canton, fared better than the Hopkins controlled areas and the others, because they are neighborhoods with their backs against the water, and raiders have only one way out, with Locust Point, which terminates in Fort McHenry National Park, being a virtual fortified position.

With the white trash priced out of the community, the protective basis for resettlement is now gone. Without nasty whites to fight the blacks at street level and with the police now exposed as enfeebled, the hunt for Whitey is on in earnest. This is how I have lived my life, as a white hunted by blacks across an urban crimescape, what H.L Mencken famously called, "the ruins of a once great medieval city."

I'd have to say, that I'm glad to have some company!

Welcome aboard the hate train, Betty!

Ishmael   May 3, 2015 12:10 PM EDT

James, gentrification is taking place in the wilds and timbered places in Utah also, except its the rednecked hillbillys that are being displaced, the rich are buying all the water and land they can lay their greasy hands on, they still need the white trash from the east side of the county to run their infrastructure but we are slowly being replaced by brothers from the south, who will work for less money but take the same abuse. People like my family are retiring and moving to the more abandoned rural areas where they can live on the scraps they throw to us, the developers have not polluted with the cash they need to ruin our lifestyle. Good luck I can see the smoke in my dreams at night coming from the cities of the east as they burn to the ground.

responds: May 8, 2015 6:22 PM EDT

That was beautiful man.

Being a redneck is now being outsourced to black dudes?

Ishmael, that is a book that needs to be written!

Take care out there.

The Hamilton Tiger Dance
'Your Favorite Riot Week Memory?' A Man Question from Ethan

"James, we know you are a real smartass. I appreciate the reporting tone you have adopted for the riots but miss the weird shit. Please, what was your funniest moment of the riots for you—your favorite riot week memory?"

Ethan

On Wednesday morning at 10:00 a.m., I was taking a tour of Hamilton with Mescaline Franklin, in his muscle shirt and death metal tattoos. He was taking photographs of the surgical damage caused by the

213

professional break in crews and became enamored of a Celtic cross on Saint Dominic's church. As he took a picture I watched a large, employed, car owning black man in middle age, whip out his Johnson and piss on the side of the jewelry store where the insurance adjuster was assessing the damage.

As Mescaline and I walked on by the piss stain a deaf white panhandler stepped away from White Jesus [a homeless white guy who only wears white and has a long mane of white hair and a bushy beard of the same ghostly hue] who he was worrying for a smoke. This is one of the deaf white guys who mug women in the neighborhood, who tried to get the pizza girl last year.

When he rose to mime for a smoke from me, I looked through him as I do to all panhandlers, even if they are missing a leg and crying and walked on. Mescaline, however, engaged him in a kung fu mime dance of bizarre aspect. The young New Jersey guy was once a Hung Gar kung fu student. I smiled as I looked ahead at the horrified look on the lady who owns Kikki's Kuts [This babe has pistols and razors tattooed on her arms.], standing on the walk with her apron and scissors, her face saying, "Oh my God, the white people have gone crazy too!"

Glad that there were no cops patrolling, I stood and watched the deaf mugger/panhandler miming Mescaline's tiger dance, until they shook hands and hugged each other.

I have to say that was my funniest five minutes, although Boomy, the Nigerian cab driver, mistaking me for the last officer of the Confederate States of America and insisting that **my** "niggers were useless and out of control" and that I needed to round them up, would have to be #2.

Coming to Harm City
Attending A Baltimore Music Festival in the Wake of the Riots

"My wife and I will be attending the 2nd annual "Moonrise Festival," a 2 day electronic music concert, Saturday & Sunday, 11am to 11pm, hosted at Pimlico racetrack in August. There has been a lot of chatter (considering recent events in, and around the city) about security. Apparently many folks are considering not attending based on the fear of potential violence, mugging, who knows (?)

"My question to Baltimore's Violence Guy: Should a mass of (predominantly white suburbanites 16-30 yrs old on average) have anything to fear? If so, what should they fear? And how should they respond?"

War Drums

Andrew W.

Andrew, after what the world has witnessed in Baltimore, I imagine you are being told by any and all that taking your wife into West Baltimore, where Pimlico Race Track is situated, is foolhardy. My thoughts on this are somewhat discordant, the negro-battling white devil in me vying with the mulattress-admiring honorary African American for control of my brain. Note that every honest person in Baltimore believes these riots were the first of many, and that the media and government—attributing the riots to the death of Freddie Gray—think that throwing some cops under the proverbial city bus will assuage black rage, when in reality, every government initiative that has contributed to the racial hatred in Baltimore is still ongoing. There will be more riots in Baltimore, perhaps purely-for-profit raids on retailers close to Halloween or school events. As with the recent riots, the aims will be largely racial purging and plunder, not protest.

The White Devil Says

1. Since the riots staged by Baltimore's innocent unarmed black teens were a rousing success on every level and encouraged weak imitation of such

behavior in less violent cities, I do expect a certain element of the Harm City Hoodrat Horde to be on the lookout for any gathering of white people, particularly since the media has agreed with them that white people coming into Baltimore to enjoy cultural attractions is a violation of African American autonomy and a threat to their cultural identity.

2. Since the politicians and media continue to lie about and cover up the true extent of the damage in Baltimore, the City Government cannot be trusted to be truthful or forthcoming with the promoters of this event in terms of risk and police protection. For instance, the Mondawmin location was central to the riot because there is a large drug distribution ring working out of that area, as indicated by anomalous purchases at area retailers [garlic powder for cutting dope and the largest end of month cash purchases in the ghetto]. If there is such a syndicate based in Pimlico, it could be good or bad. They may prefer to have a bunch of white customers come to their door step and consume mass quantities of their product. Or, they may resent increased police presence, and with younger members lashing out at the cops, decide to up their street cred like the Mondawmin-based crews did.

What I'm pointing out here is how important the promoter is in assessing the situation. The best case scenario is they provide private security, preferably a biker gang or Guardian Angels, whose presence will not ignite anti-police feelings.

3. If some hoodrat gets his neck broken by the cops just before this event, then going into Pimlico would be suicide.

The Honorary African American Says

1. Blacks who live around Pimlico benefit from the race track through employment there and by charging a small fee for motorists to park in their driveways, in front of their house, and even on their lawn, much like the Waverly area residents worked as valets and parking lot attendants when Memorial Stadium was open on 33rd Street. Pimlico is not seen as a product of gentrification as Orioles Park at Camden Yards is. When Memorial Stadium was vacated by the Orioles Waverly area residents lost income and then the yuppies moved into upscale housing that replaced the park and raised the tax bill on the locals. So, while some 'white'

event set in Camden Yards or in Waverly might draw black ire, Pimlico is a longstanding cultural institution enjoyed by many blacks who like to bet on the horses, which benefits the locals. [Note: Erique lives in Pimlico and says that event goers are the problem, partying on family stoops and getting violent coming from the events drunk.]

2. The Baltimore riots were fueled by cohesive large scale mobs exiting their criminal training ground, where they are prepared for a lifetime of illiteracy and incarceration: Baltimore City Schools. These riots only reached virulent levels during the week. The media claims that the riots calmed down after Friday because of the police indictments, but this was not so. Friday was as hot as any day of the riots other than Monday. The first riots on the Saturday following the death of Freddie Gray were not a fraction of what came on Monday after his funeral. Recall that all parties predicted that the funeral would calm tensions, not considering that Freddie Gray's death was just an excuse to vent long standing hatreds, and that proper mass riots could not be organized until high school was in session. When another weekend rolled around, there was

no longer an ability to marshal large ghetto forces, absent their high school breeding grounds. The media coverage was a complete lie and a hoax, the rioters have been excused, and the race-purging strike teams in outlying areas ignored or covered up. During the school year, attend such events in Baltimore only on the weekend. If they have a Friday night event, do not go. As this event is in August, I predict there will be minimal problems.

3. If parking will not be adequate at the race track, do not take public transportation! Never take a white woman onto Baltimore public transportation—ever! All of the worst black mob attacks on whites in Baltimore [outside of a riot context] were triggered by the presence of a white woman. If there is not adequate parking, go out in July, into the adjacent neighborhood, and arrange to park on a home owner's property, being certain to exchange contact information and a promise to pay above his normal rate so that he won't sell your spot to some other white guy while your wife is making you late as she dyes her hair all the colors of the rainbow.

4. Travel with a group that consists of at least three men and no more than 3 women. Ideally you have a bachelor or two with you. Make sure you are not

traveling with any loud assholes or belligerent drunks.

5. Talk to the promoter about security precautions. You need to know what he has arranged and what his staff will look like.

6. Wear wide-rimmed hats and keep ski caps in a pocket or fanny pack, in case your group gets stoned by neighborhood kids. A bush hat with a knit hat underneath will help a lot when bottles and stones start to fly.

7. If this is a field seating event, carry a mix of light-framed lawn chairs to be used as shields by your women and folding metal chairs to be used as pro-wrestling weapons by the men. The folding metal chair can be used as a pole axe or a thrusting ram, depending on whether you hold it by both legs or by the back and the bar.

8. As for tactics, observe the video on the article 'Man Down' in which a phalanx of city cops assault a hood rat position in city side streets not unlike the area surrounding Pimlico. If attacked you want to organize like the hood rats, and not the cops. The cops did everything wrong. You want an organized retreat. Whoever is attacking is operating from a

base of community support and ammunition in the form of rocks, bottles etc. Do not run, but walk backwards, holding your lawn chairs as shields and watching your flanks, until the aggressors break off, and they will. The farther you get from the scene of the initial attack, the less community support they will get and the more likely it will be that a resident will come to your aid. Keep in mind that it was middle aged black men, not white cops, who saved white people in the streets this past week.

9. Finally, if the event is held between the 1st [SSI distribution] and the 16th [last EBT distribution] the ghetto will be flush with government money. Any event held after the 20th will be likely to draw criminal predators, mostly teens ranging away from the nest to fill their mother's requests, such as, "Baby, get me a new purse—a nice leather one like those white ladies carry."

Young man, I don't normally party with psychedelic music freaks, but when I do, I do it Harm City, where the war drums down by the river reverberate through the asphalt jungle and rise up to heaven on a piteous waft of despair, to warm my cold heart with the woe of the downtrodden.

Enjoy!

Andrew W.   May 4, 2015 12:04 PM EDT

Extra details / thoughts:

The event will be on the 8th and 9th. +1 for the young cracker couple.

Not having been to the debut event last year, I am still 100% positive (based on past festival-going experience) that the security will be handled by a private firm, such as CSC (the mostly un-athletic and un-intimidating guys and gals in yellow & black uniforms), or the like. Their primary weapon is a walkie-talkie. They are there to pat-down white kids sneaking in capsules, and probably for insurance purposes. No matter their numbers, they are always grossly outnumbered by attendees, at least 100 to 1.

I have a feeling that there will be (at least a minimal) BPD presence. Municipals are always on call with these events (use the antiquated term 'rave' if you will), because you see James the city realizes that:

A) these concerts are the hottest shit right now and bring in tall stacks of cash, so as a broke-ass city you simply can't ignore them, and

B) it's the world's biggest open-air drug market. Oh, did I mention that? That hundreds (maybe thousands, who knows) of white teens/young adults will be attempting to solicit party drugs from strangers? Don't believe me? Look into the Merriweather incident (county! all Columbia kids!) from last year. It's the biggest fear for promoters and the municipality: overdoses and their political aftermath.

Last year's event went down without a hitch apparently. But Freddie Gray was still slingin' dat good molly back then, and Baltimore was a 'city on the rebound'.

Private vehicular transportation to/fro seems to be the order of the day here.

responds: May 6, 2015 12:45 PM EDT

I think that if there is expected to be a lot of drug use, that there will be no small or large scale attacks by local blacks of the criminal sort, as they will be busy providing customer service. There will, however, be some opportunistic violence and stick ups on the perimeter, mostly targeting the intoxicated while they leave.

'A Time for Men'

An Epilogue to War Drums: 40 Miles from the Big House: Freddie Ruiz Steps Into the Mangina Breach

I have noticed that many libertarians and masculinity advocates in their 30s and 40s are hoping for civil unrest and government breakdown so that men may once against find a place in society along traditional lines, as protectors, as the strength of a family, or the autonomous drivers of a business. I have been writing **War Drums: 40 Miles From The Big House** during the course of the riots and am wrapping the project up today, to serve as a case study for the disintegration of mid-sized cities to come.

226

Over this past week, as Baltimore Society broke down very apocalyptically we had the following effects:

1. The delinquent students of a single high school won a marginal victory against the entire Baltimore City police department!

2. All police assets from Baltimore City and surrounding municipalities were concentrated in three zones, leaving over 95% of Baltimore City and Baltimore County without police protection.

3. News coverage outside of the political/police zone was zero, leaving the citizens utterly blind except for websites like this and social media. Face to face interaction among men once again became important.

4. Lone white women away from home were targeted for gang rape by gangs of black men immediately across the city and county.

5. Commercial districts and residential areas were patrolled by gangs of 5-15 mature black men with clubs, unopposed by police but easily deterred by the two gun-armed white men who stood up to them. The professional gun-armed black criminals

were staging home invasions, drug stash-house raids, and stealthy break-ins of high value targets under cover of darkness and were not present as officers with the bully packs, as they were in Rwanda, making these incursion teams shy away from organized and/or gun-armed white men.

6. Approximately 12 murders were reported on social media and are, just now—a week later— being looked into by police and the media. I theorize that as many additional drug gang executions and assassinations took place during this period, and that the riots and zero police presence outside of the riot zones has facilitated easy disposal of the bodies and blocked any effective investigation. It seems likely to infer that the three gangs that organized these riots: the Cripps, Bloods and Black Guerilla Family, have strengthened themselves at the expense of rival crews, which may therefore alter the scope of the next round of unrest in ways I could only guess at.

7. Over 200 businesses [over 300 hundred claimed losses], including at least 13 pharmacies and up to a third of liquor stores, have been wiped from the face of the earth, many of them minority businesses which are uninsured and will not recover. This places the drug gangs in a position to expand the

illegal economy in areas where businesses will not return—as they did not return after the 1968 riots—which offsets losses of territory recently suffered at the hands of Johns Hopkins Hospital and University buying up drug territory.

8. Black criminals now know that when a peaceful demonstration or riot occurs in the future, that whatever crimes they deem to commit will be unopposed by police, so expect more aggressive and more immediate corollary attacks in outlying areas in the next round of unrest.

9. The police, politicians and media have attributed the entire episode to a symptom [the death of Freddie Gray] rather than a cause, and can be expected to be taken unawares in the future as they begin to believe their own lies.

10. All whites I have spoken to have noted that blacks they normally come into contact with have been behaving with increased—or not before present—hostility. This has been noted by the author as well, with hard eye-contact and aggressive posturing evidenced by most black males I now encounter, where before that was a minority expression of about a third of such men.

Stepping Into The Mangina Breach

Freddie Ruiz is a young Mexican martial artist, who has served as a sparring partner for one of my fighters. He arrived in the U.S. in the wake of civil unrest in his own country which claimed the life of his Uncle, who was a small business owner executed by a drug gang for not paying protection money. While attending a Washington D.C. area high school he was attacked by three larger black students with bats. He used a knife to maim one attacker and discourage the other two, and has since moved to Baltimore, married the daughter of one of my coaches, and had a son.

Freddie was scheduled to attend my stick-fighting seminar this past Sunday. His father-in-law informed me of Freddie's reason for not attending.

Freddie worked as a simple clerk for a chain or retailers that was hit hard by break-in crews, door-crashing squads of gun-armed gangsters, and mobs of teens. He was employed at a distant upscale suburban location. When a number of inner city locations run by women, sissy white men, and timid black men were lost, his company did an internal search for Real Men, a decidedly taboo act in postmodern sissy America.

Within two days, Freddie was armored with a bullet-proof vest, licensed to carry a firearm, armed with a 9mm auto, and promoted to 'Regional Manager!'

This kind of elevation of young men normally only occurs on battlefields or on sports teams—not in sissy, civilized, shop keeping society.

The leaders and academics of our sick corrupt society have labored for nearly two centuries to emasculate our young men from the cradle to the grave.

I now observe, through what of my primal man's eye I have been able to salvage from this systematic assault on my humanity, that all it takes is a few urban savages to rip the mask away from the slave mistress that owns us to expose her for the impotent, squabbling bitch that she is and open the door for men to be men once again, as the lie that encases our souls crumbles to dust with every fumbling falsehood that falls flat beneath the reality of naked force. The hooting black heathens that have hunted me in the streets of Baltimore for over 30 years might be my enemies, but they at least acknowledge my manhood as they probe for my every weakness and have struck a resounding blow against the slave mistress society that seeks with its every apparatus to render me weak to the point of meek.

The Enemy of My Enemy is Still My Enemy, and I recognize his achievement, even as I prepare to oppose him.

Zach   May 14, 2015 5:48 AM EDT

Baltimore Riots remind me so much of the Braşov Rebellion. The government realized that they would have a big PR problem if they prosecuted the participants as they normally would. Within two years, governments all through the Eastern Bloc were in the process of a radical transformation to appease the emboldened population. Didn't matter. Two years later, the whole region overthrew their oppressors.

In that case, it was a good thing. If this happens today, it will be thanks to imagined oppression.

responds: May 16, 2015 6:30 PM EDT

Emboldened is what I am seeing on the ground.

Since the riots, instead of steeling on the sly, black shoplifters are now walking up to my bosses and telling them to get out of the way as they carry merchandize out the door.

The Return of Men?
Aftermath: War Drums: Forty Miles From The Big House

On Saturday and Sunday, as the curfew was lifted and the National Guard rolled out of the battered economic node of Baltimore—now diminished by 200 businesses—the mood among whites was generally that of anxious fear of blacks. Meanwhile, blacks I encountered were more likely to be hostile, and more intensely hostile, than usual.

Today I took an extra two hours returning from my night job and walked by circuitous paths to the locations where I documented events over the course of the last week: the block where Emanuel stopped the bat-armed black men with a leveled pistol, the deserted transfer point where I met

Columbine Joe, the businesses that were looted, and the school bus that would be occupied by boys of the same age as those who fought the BPD to a standstill—boys who must feel empowered and imperiled by association.

From work to home, over the course of 15 hours, I was in close contact with 123 people, including the 48 on the 'school' bus. The breakdown at work was predominantly white, while on the bus it was overwhelmingly black. On foot it was predominantly black. I did not parse the numbers, just kept a running count of bodies within low voice and close eye contact range.

The mood had shifted once again; it was no longer the rage and worry of the riots, the fear and hostility of the wind down, nor the studied alienation if the normal Harm City day. Below are my observations of the following types of people behaving abnormally toward me.

Conservative and working class whites have finally achieved anger and have voiced hostile feeling towards blacks in general, with many now convinced that their grandparents had been right all along, that blacks are nothing but savage opportunistic predators. These whites are now acting like the blacks did two days ago.

White Liberals are all over the place, from hope to despair, seemingly in different stages of redefining or doing mental back-flips to reaffirm their contrived world.

Notably, I am one of only two whites on foot in the county or the city within my sight from 8:30 a.m. to 12:00 p.m.

The blacks?

Only one black youth swaggered menacingly at me today, while four held doors for me or addressed me as, "sir." Normally door holding by black youth is a twice annual occurrence, and apish posturing is a daily constant.

Numerous black ladies and girls went out of their way to smile and wave and say good morning, almost as if they were glad to see this hobbling white devil with the shaved head and out of season beard.

When I boarded the bus, where the vast majority of blacks normally spread out or place their bags on the seat next to them in order to deny a seat or generate a confrontation, none did so on the #55 at 8:45 a.m. The rap music that is usually turned up as soon as a white person sits down did not scream its pedestrian obscenities across the racial divide.

No one attempted to sit next to me—which is normal, even though I always leave space.

As I rose to a stop too soon to give a boy with his hand in a cast a seat, his friends opened the door for me, and I informed them that I was getting off at the next stop. Meanwhile, the high school teacher, a man of 35, who has accompanied these boys on their way to school as a kind of chaperon begins fielding questions about the shirt I am wearing, a Pick Your Fights Promotions t-shirt I was given after losing via arm bar to Damien Kestle in a pipe versus chain bout in Virginia Beach in 2009.

As the two tall boys open the door for me and I thank them, the man begins explaining about the promotion and that I am a coach, and I wonder if I know him as the bus pulls off and I shoulder my pack.

As I walk the neighborhood on a lopsided grid observing who is out and about and their attitude, I do wonder about the fact that this was the first of about two dozens of rides on that time slot school bus in which a man engaged male youths in conversation rather than just thumbing his smart phone while they pretended to be men.

As I finally return to my block, I notice a tall dainty looking black girl, of about 20 years, who always dresses in professional attire and is usually walking alone past my house from the same bus stop. I have always kept my distance and tried not to glance at her, in order to keep from frightening her, as it is normally just her and me on these side streets. Fortunately I am usually beat from work and she has long legs so I can let her pass me by. Her destination is across the street, where she either visits or lives with a young white man, who looks good for nothing more strenuous than lead guitar work.

Today, he has walked the mile to greet her and is returning to his/their house holding her hand. They both nod at me, apparently cheered to see me. This is my first definitive man sighting on White Avenue in five years.

Maybe—I wish, but still, maybe—men and women are waking up to the fact that the heavily armed law enforcement organization whose officers parade in 'protect and serve' attire, meant what its leaders said when they told the citizens of Baltimore that they were on their own; that the police could barely protect their own.

Survivalist expert, James Wesley, Rawles, in How To Survive The End of The World as We Know It, _**'One Tank Of Gas Away'**_, surmised that police departments would attempt to protect civilians and keep order in times of unrest, but that these efforts would disintegrate as officers moved off to take care of their own families. I found this a reasonable supposition. I do not recall any other writers on such affairs predicting that the police, in times of crises, would immediately and totally abandon the bottom 99% of the population to whatever force assailed them.

Perhaps we owe those Mondawmin hoodrats a debt, for waking the sleep walkers among us—like this fellow who has let the frail willowy girl walk a mile and a half through a moderately high crime urban area, which hosts over a dozen half way houses for criminals, perverts and drug addicts—up to the fact that men have a natural duty to their women and their young, and to the men they align with, and that if this sense of duty is absent totally, then we are all just meat waiting to be skewered on the government spit and roasted over the criminal fire.

guest   May 5, 2015 7:08 PM EDT

Speaking of crisis, I highly recommend:

< a href="https://web.archive.org/web/20120706120 624/http://sovietoutpost.revdisk.org/?p=72">Wor ds from a Bosnian Survivalist</a>

"I am from Bosnia. You know, between 1992 and 1995 it was hell (war). For one year I lived, and survived, in a city with 6000 people, without water, electricity, gasoline, medical help, civil defense, distribution service, any kind of traditional service or centralized rule.

Our city was blockaded by the army and for 1 year life in the city turned into total crap. We had no army, no police, we only had armed groups – those armed protected their homes and families."

And <a href="http://bayourenaissanceman.blogspot.com/ 2008/08/lessons-learned-from-hurricanes-katrina.html">Lessons learned from Hurricanes Katrina and Rita</a>

Both must reads!

responds: May 8, 2015 5:42 PM EDT

Thank you so much for the links.

I will check them out.

Glad you made it out the other end of that mess.

Jim Fry   May 5, 2015 6:20 PM EDT

An initial perspective on reading Rawles: He appears to be on key on most aspects and facets of speculating the textures and flavors of the collapse scenarios. One minor nuance is he recommends excess resources be parked in precious metals. I disagree, having contemplated this deeply, inasmuch as water purification devices, bullets, condoms, booze, smokes and similar will have greater recognized value once fiscal and societal paradigms shift. While navigating preparations and the slow grind and wealth transfers (fraud in markets and paper) currently underway, metals and cash in hand make perfect sense (as they have the least amount of fees/tax/fraud), but not so much later when cash may devalue to zero and silver will be most important if hunting werewolves!

I know, speculative, yet we need to find some foundation for discerning or divining the future.

JL

responds: May 8, 2015 5:45 PM EDT

I don't have a financial mind. I once asked a 12 year old to do my taxes and he told me to hire an accountant.

Condoms as money—that's huge—and they are packaged to fit in a wallet and replace that devalued cash.

Thanks Jim.

Jim Fry   May 5, 2015 5:15 PM EDT

James,

Thank you for the salient survival book recommendation. In reading the One Tank Away piece I'm reminded of salon conversations my brother and I have regularly.

I've been a power engineer and project manager my whole career and what few recognize well is the fragile nature of the US electrical grid which will deeply impact all ability to retain cooling on nuclear plants. This is the single factor I've never resolved regarding end of time we've known scenarios. It simply ends bad and the only reason I'm not a cheerleader for collapse.

Without discounting the suffering and impacts

collapse would cause 99.99% of everyone, most of the factors have a variety of ways they may be navigated, negotiated and presumable (partially) mitigated, excluding the multiple nuclear catastrophe facet. Without impaling myself on either exuberant faux hope or upon exaggerated doom, I'm still left with the sense that on the nuclear card, we're all ... screwed ...

Handling this resolution without falling into a depressive state and stance is my greatest challenge, which I combat by resolving that the best I may do is be generally kind, helpful and giving to those I care about and encounter. None of us know for certain if we have more lives or consciousness when we pass from this story, but I do get a sense that we may be continually refined across life and that there may be more to come, beyond, so (if so) why waste the course we're in, no matter how arduous it may be at times?

responds: May 8, 2015 5:51 PM EDT

It seems we're on the same metaphysical page Jim.

Okay, the nuclear thing scares the shit out of me. I'm okay wearing dirty animal hides, but I don't want to glow.

Could you write us an article about

243

that and email it to
jameslafond.com@gmail.com? I can
send any pdfs you want as
compensation. I have pdfs of all the
print books. Just tell me what titles you
want.

Take care, Jim.

Hoodrat Reading List
A Harm City Librarian Brings to Light the Secret Wisdom of the Ghetto: Appendix to War Drums

For your white bigots and elitist liberals out there who think that blacks are hopelessly sub-literate, and hence either turn rightward in disgust or extend the guilt ridden patronizing hand of the left, I have acquired what one might call the Harm City reading list, compiled by a librarian who was saddened that I even asked and only complied with the request out of respect for my status as a published author.

The lack of capitalization in titles and names is courtesy of the library system database. I thought we should keep it.

1. Dopeman: memoirs of a snitch by JaQuavis.

2. Eviction notice: a hood rat novel by K'wan.

3. In my hood 3 by Endy.

4. Thug in me by Williams, Karen.

5. Bitch, part 1 by King, Deja. [I think there is a bitch reloaded, also.]

6. Down ass bitch: part 1 by Bandz, Lola.

7. B-more careful by Holmes, Shannon.

8. Riding dirty on I-95: a novel by Turner, Nikki.

9. Candy licker an urban erotic tale by Noire.

10. Street life by Jihad.

11. Little ghetto girl by Santiago, Danielle.

12. Chyna Black: a novel by Ervin, Keisha.

13. Payback is a mutha by Clark, Wahida.

14. The ski mask way by 50 Cent (Musician)

15. The boss ...: the story of a female hustler by Tysha.

Mrs. Emerson, if you could please schedule me an interview with the author known as Noire— providing she is, and has always been, a she—I would be glad to have a face to face discussion about her work.

Thank you.

Celine   May 8, 2015 5:06 PM EDT

Dear Mr. LaFond,

I read through your list twice trying to decide if it was real or something you were making up, like those joke titles from when I was a kid, "The Yellow River," by I.P. Standing...

Best guess: You're having fun again with your sharp wit?

Just wondering,

Celine

responds: May 8, 2015 5:40 PM EDT

My suspicious lady,

These titles were provided by a Baltimore City librarian, who did not include 'Bitch reloaded' as a matter of taste I think.

And don't you worry, I will write my own urban novel, The Legend of Lesbo Jones.

'My Peoples'

**Country Boy 2: Still Country, The Aftermath, by
Allen Little and Blake Karrington**

2011, 58 pages, set in 10 point type with 1 inch
margins

One's confidence in a book is shaken somewhat
when the title is misspelled on the 104 word
dustcover, and that it is accompanied by another
misspelling.

When one turns to the interior page and sees that
the publisher has not properly spaced the names of
the authors, one begins to suspect the publisher,
rather than the author.

When the reader then discovers that the type has been set in 10 point and the page count was beefed up by using extra wide margins, that line drop errors have not been corrected, and that basic editing such as separating dialog from narrative, and using uniform line breaks and spacing in the text, then the publisher is indicted in the mind's eye and one feels better about reading the author's story.

It is not necessary to read Country Boy, as back story is woven in nicely upon the introduction of key characters, and not in a fashion that would spoil the first book if the reader is of a mind to try it.

The main characters are Q, who is only addressed by his 'government name' of Quentel, by the authorities, and his vicious killer babe Van, who has a pit bull and a 9mm. The government has screwed up on Q's case by mishandling evidence and he is being released by a judge that knows he is guilty. This big body beautiful country boy is now set to take out the upstart gangster that took over his drug territory while Van and her girls torture and kill the male and female snitches who put him behind bars.

The cast is large and varied, the story has a good pace, and the violence is not overdone. I disagree with how the author spelled some ebonic terms, but that is a quibbling matter of ghetto scholarship best settled over a forty and some lake trout. The following is a sample of the moral gravity of the urban fiction genre from page 39:

"That's the way niggas get popped, trying to get a cheaper price."

What I liked about the setting was the ghetto mindset that 'the government' is the enemy, a vast faceless machine that the criminals are at war with. Country Boy is Bonnie and Clyde for the 21st Century marginally literate urbanite. The violence and the sex are not over done, much of it being inferred. This has the effect of maintaining the nihilistic perspective in the reader's mind, as opposed to jarring the reader into disassociating himself from a nihilistic spectacle.

Reading Country Boy 2 was not the wasted hour that I expected, but an entertaining glance at society through the hate-filled lens shared by roughly 5% of American society. If you read Country Boy 2, keep in mind that approximately 15

million humans see our world through the jaded-in-
youth eyes of Q and Van.

The Discipline of Stone
Columbine Joe! #6

"His was the discipline of Steel!"

-Conan the Barbarian

In the wake of the G-man Affair I sought counsel on behalf of junior hoodrats from a man whose spent his fair share on the wrong side of the law, and unlike the predictably short-lived G-man, is still alive and kicking.

Although the actual attacks on Baltimore and its inmates by the hoodrat brigades had to do with long standing hatreds and had nothing to do with the fate of G-man, as reported by the Slaves of the Lie—G-man's death did have the effect of giving over the tainted media stage to The Lie.

Of the entire sorry episode, the most absurd aspect had to be the end of G-man. It was like dropping a rabbit down in front of a pack of hounds. Even though the rabbit had no reason to run, other than habit, it ran. And even though the hounds had not come to get this rabbit—well, that's what they do! Who was a bigger idiot, the guy that ran from the cops on principle, or the guys that chased out of sheer habit?

Class, Stoner Joe Says:

Look, the least rational thing you can do when living the life is run from the cops. Really, they have helicopters, dogs, vehicles and they will beat you ass for making them run those doughnuts off. Everyone knows that when you run from the cops you get your punishment. The most absolute and long standing dictum of being on the wrong side of the law is—don't run. It is very rare that the cops have their act together enough to even make a charge stick. They're just out there racking up drug arrest stats like state troopers writing tickets, because that's what they do.

I have run from the cops but not to be a dick. That is an important distinction. If they don't have a good eye on me, like this time I was getting high down by the train tracks, I'll run, and I did. Then I heard the officer call, "Mister Henley, come back here please. I know where you live."

Oh yeah, that! Well, as much as that sucks, what is the point in making this guy work his ass off? He is after all just doing his job, such as it is.

In my present life, working as a Christian missionary, I use such stories to illustrate various aspects of life to people, who, should we say, might not normally be inclined to listen. I personally found that when dealing with the cops, humor goes a long way.

One time a friend and I were walking to the Dunkin' Doughnuts out in Reisterstown. That place was a change for us Essex boys. The cops around here are known to kick your ass—look what they have to deal with. But those boys, they were cool. The ironic thing is the Dunkin' Doughnuts is packed with cops—which is a laugh all in itself—and we're walking towards it smoking a blunt.

My friend's smoking and I see this cop pulling over behind us and say, "Toke it, swallow it!"

So he chokes that blunt down, gone, end of problem, right. The cop then greets us—nice enough and all—and calls us over. My friend is having a hard time—this blunt is not all the way down. The cop asks him if he's okay as he's kind of leaning forward next to the cop car. He goes to say something—I don't know what, because it was lost in the moment—and then coughs out this massive pungent smoke ball right into the cop's car, into the cop's face!

AS, THE, DRUG, USER, it is incumbent upon you to remain cool. This is not the time to be a dick, not the time to run, and definitely not the time to give this guy any shit. You realize he's already going to have to deal with his supervisor smelling him and saying, "So Johnson, what have you been doing on your lunch break?"

I just smiled and said, "Oh, we are well, thank you, officer."

The cop was cool—said, "How about if you boys take this indoors?"

Of course, the cop has to have a sense of humor for this to work or you have a knee in your back, and sometimes it is so.

War Drums

One time I had just been huffing and I'm driving down the road when this cop pulls me over. Now this is over here in Essex where aggressive policing is the way, so you want to do what you can to lighten his day.

The cop is standing next to the door and he knows this is not a drunk driving situation. No alcohol smell, no bottles. I'm not drunk. But the eyes do not lie. He looks at me and says, "Son, are you high?"

I just responded, "Well Sir, I was until you pulled me over. I can tell you that I was not driving at the time, and that your evidence is unfortunately gone."

He laughed outright at that. It was a great ice breaker and definitely helped me manage the situation I found myself in. Like most people, cops do not want to have to spend their time dealing with those who lie right to their face as a matter of principal. Now, there are times when the truth must not be told when you're on the other side. But the habit of lying or running builds animosity, and there is little value to building animosity to your cause in the minds of those in power.

'From Time's Booby-Trapped Vagina'

Long White Con by Iceberg Slim: Appendix to War Drums

2011, Cash Money Content,158 pages

In the late 1960s Iceberg Slim wrote Pimp, about which he was interviewed on network television. He then wrote Trick Baby, about the rise of a con man Johnny O'Brian, named White Folks, who was "the blue-eyed, white-skinned nigger con man from the Big Windy," who had been mentored by black Blue Howard.

The White Folks novels comprise a tutorial on how to get over on the white man by turning his own rigged game against him. Although the period jargon is not the same, and Johnny O'Brian, and Iceberg Slim for that matter, would not even rate as gangsters in today's game, Long White Con is an expose of the enemy of the author's people, the multilayered corporate/political/law-enforcement/criminal system. In many ways this is little different from other novels and movies of the same era obsessed with stings, heists, and big cons—like a black 1970s Oceans Eleven.

A key way Long White Con pays it truer than standard fare in the genre is the narrative device of regarding the subject of the rip-off as simply "the mark" through most of the story. He is not even regarded as human by the narrative voice. This book was written by a social predator, who understood that a whore was only a whore and not a person, as was "the mark."

For example, in The Naked Soul of Iceberg Slim the author declares, "I suddenly realized that I had lost all power over her and therefore in her cold-blooded whore judgment I was just another customer, a chump john."

Consider that the young gangsters that trained the thugs, who mentored the thugs, who directed the recent Baltimore riots and purges, having predicted the establishments every move, very likely used the writings of Iceberg Slim—or an author or rapper influenced by him—to gain an understanding of the vulnerabilities of the liberal white slave system that was brought to its knees by a mob of high school children—none of whom will be charged or tried for a crime.

Johnny O'Brian is a fun character, and a good window on the parasitic world. But the best part of this book is the preface, in which Iceberg Slim is saved by White Folks in the nick of time, just as "Big Apple rotten, glossy and slick as ermine droppings," a "ho" reporter from new York who was flown out to interview Slim in LA, was setting him up for a rape charge, and a beating by the LAPD, just to get a story, because that's how the white establishment rolls.

I leave you with one typical line from Iceberg Slim, concerning this curvaceous white woman seemingly designed to entrap black man in a sex scandal, and launched across 3,000 miles at a former pimp minding his own business.

"She handcuffed her breath for an instant. You know, like one of those closet bisexual whores in

Long Island emoting snob outrage at the visual atrocity of some lackey peasant sneaking a crap in the shrubbery."

If you would like to understand the depth of black American antipathy toward "the system" and would also like to be entertained by some slick offbeat prose, try Iceberg Slim.

Jim Fry   May 12, 2015 10:43 PM EDT

Salient & Sage:

There is no judgment here, simply strategy exposed:

"Consider that the young gangsters that trained the thugs, who mentored the thugs, who directed the recent Baltimore riots and purges, having predicted the establishments every move, very likely used the writings of Iceberg Slim—or an author or rapper influenced by him—to gain an understanding of the vulnerabilities of the liberal white slave system that was brought to its knees by a mob of high school children—none of whom will be charged or tried for a crime."

"Directed" + "predicted" + "vulnerabilities" + "slave system" + "brought to its kness" = *TRUTH* ...

 **responds:** May 16, 2015 6:39 PM EDT

This guy could really write. I was impressed, and glad you liked the review Jim—I pretty much stumble through them and hope it works.

Dialog with a Large Suburban Brain

A Certified Thinker Plumbs the Violence Guy Gray Matter

I was speaking to Daniel, a concerned, upscale dude who graduated from MIT with a degree in something I can't quite grasp. He was asking me about the recent unrest in Harm City as he drove me across town. Toward the end of our drive he asked me for a concise cause.

I replied, "The drug war is a war on the underclass, therefore you have an alienated and restive underclass—the police force is an army of occupation, an under strength army."

Daniel continued. "I can see what you mean. I ran in the D.C. Marathon last weekend, and the police who secured the route were all very polite, helpful, professional—until this one officer ignored a traffic signal and nearly hit me. I yelled at him, 'Hey, that's against the law! You can't do that.'"

"He then stopped and addressed me in manner that was chilling in its menace. Sure, he was only one cop out of the bunch, but, in his mind, he was above the law and very willing to impose his lawless will on a person of the class he is ostensibly serving and protecting. So I could well imagine if I were a low income kind of guy how bad it could be. So your point is that this is probably one of those cops active in—and therefore callused by—this war on drugs?"

"Yes, it becomes a culture. A culture does not require full participation for its norms to be imposed."

"Norms, which, in this case, constitute a culture of intimidation?"

"A necessary culture of intimidation if a small number of cops are to impose their will on a relatively vast underclass."

"Okay, so what is the solution?"

"I don't believe in solutions."

"I am sick of hearing that. You have named a concise cause, so name a concise solution."

"Okay, send me back in time—you can surely build a time machine—so that I can murder William Bradford and his Pilgrims when they land at Plymouth Bay. That ought to nix the drug war, and prohibition."

"Yes, prohibition was such a roaring success it is astonishing that we walked into this 'War on Drugs' so wide eyed. Thanks for the food for thought."

"Thanks for the ride Daniel, and please, don't mouth off to a Baltimore city cop—okay."

Jeremy Bentham   May 17, 2015 3:55 PM EDT

Yes James, there is still the unexpected, isn't there? LOL! What I find rather astonishing is that Daniel actually imagined that the D.C. police officer would quietly accept a rebuke from him instead of immediately becoming hostile. Even in small towns cops don't accept criticism gladly, particularly from impecunious members of the citizenry. What a cop whom I know once told me was that what he liked about working in law enforcement was that "the customer is always wrong". But I guess I should not be surprised. Talking back to authority figures is clearly a white millennial generation thing, just as much as it is a black ghetto thing, in its own way. We white Baby Boomer and Gen X types generally discovered that John Cougar Mellencamp was correct: "when I fight authority, authority always wins". There are times when discretion is the better part of valor; best to just keep your mouth shut over the petty injustices of life inflicted on you by the powerful and connected. On the other hand, if the cop running the light had hit the young man, he would have really had something to complain about; he could have also sued the city for huge sums of money because of the cop's negligence. In that case go for it!

As for the law of unintended consequences, I think on close inspection we will find that many of these consequences were neither unintended nor unforeseen. The Woman needs chaos to get the public's support for her radical transformation of American society. The Woman doesn't really care about the collateral damage caused by her polices. The media will help her cover them up. Even should anyone in the public notice the harm done, The Woman has always been able to blame it all on the Republicans, uncaring Conservatives, racist white people, etc. It's all about gaining more power and control for The Woman over people's lives.

Consequently we Conservatives have come to mistrust authority as well, much more than you might think. Even then we don't see anything to be gained by demonizing the police. In fact Conservatives believe our cities need more police officers on the streets, but public safety isn't a high priority with The Woman.

It isn't just happening in this country. Radical Leftists are also working diligently in the other English speaking countries to "transform" their cultures. John J. Ray of Australia has chronicled this on his various blog sites.

"I record on this blog many examples of negligent, inefficient and reprehensible behavior on the part of British police. After 13 years of Labour party rule they have become highly politicized, with values that reflect the demands made on them by the political Left rather than what the community expects of them. They have become lazy and cowardly and avoid dealing with real crime wherever possible—preferring instead to harass normal decent people for minor infractions— particularly offences against political correctness. They are an excellent example of the destruction that can be brought about by Leftist meddling."

"I also record on this blog much social worker evil—particularly British social worker evil. The evil is neither negligent nor random. It follows exactly the pattern you would expect from the

Marxist-oriented indoctrination they get in social work school—where the middle class is seen as the enemy and the underclass is seen as virtuous. So social workers are lightning fast to take children away from normal decent parents on the basis of minor or imaginary infractions while turning a blind eye to gross child abuse by the underclass." - John J. Ray (M.A.; Ph.D.) Brisbane, Australia, Political Correctness Watch, Dissecting Leftism BlogSpot.

"Until you accept that the aim of Leftists is to hurt, not help, none of their actions makes sense."

-John J. Ray (M.A.; Ph.D.) Brisbane, Australia, Dissecting Leftism BlogSpot

Jeremy Bentham   May 13, 2015 2:19 PM EDT

So this guy goes to the doctor and says "Doctor, I keep getting these terrible hang-overs. Is there something I can do to prevent them?" The Doctor replies. "Yes, quit drinking so much alcohol." "No really Doc, be serious!" the man says," What can I do to stop these hangovers?"

responds: May 16, 2015 6:38 PM EDT

He even brought up 'the law of unintended consequences' and still wanted to find a solution.

I depressed him, I think.

Jeremy Bentham   May 13, 2015 1:59 PM EDT

Hey James, I'm reminded of my high school days. Back then female students would occasionally ask the young men on the wrestling squad for advice on weight loss. The young ladies imagined, that given the constant struggle the wrestlers engaged in to make weight in order to compete, they must know some clever tricks on how to lose weight quickly. The wrestlers would invariably answer that the process of making weight was pretty simple and straight forward: don't eat and work out vigorously. However, none of the young ladies found this advice to be at all helpful. It was not the solution they wanted to hear. Likewise I'm sure that when you say you "don't believe in solutions" James, many people think that is a cop out. But really, what do people expect to hear from a contrarian crackpot like yourself James? LOL!

In your defense, the fact is at this point in time there are NO solutions to our social problems. At least none that everyone in our presently divided "multicultural" country will find acceptable and palatable. We are not even in agreement on what constitutes a societal problem or not. Consequently we will likely remain at an impasse on even the most threatening issues until something falls apart and forces us to act in some way.

Anyway, even then, given our lack of ability agree on anything, we are probably as likely to pick an ineffective or even counter-productive course of action as an effective one. The fact that many Americans still imagine that the Republicans and the Democrats can still be made to work together illustrates the depth of their self-delusion. That is akin to being a German in 1932 and expecting the National Socialist, Communist and Social Democrat parties to all work together for the "greater good". In reality the Communists and National Socialists would have destroyed the Social Democrats and then turned on each other.

The Communists and National Socialists would never have ceased trying to destroy each other and establish one-party rule of their country, since in their paradigms they alone represented the "greater good". The Communists and the National Socialists were each completely anti-democratic, so even if they could have found reason to work together, would a coalition totalitarian oligarchy have been any less unpleasant than a one-party ruled totalitarian state? Similarly, if the Republicans and Democrats, as both parties are constituted today, ever decide to work together hand in hand in total harmony, you can kiss any notions of you have of freedom, self-determination and unalienable civil rights goodbye forever!

FYI, the War on Drugs has its origins way back in the Prohibition era. Prior to the passage of the federal Harrison Act of 1914 one could buy heroin, opium, cocaine and marijuana at your local apothecary or general store. Both the prohibition of drugs and of alcohol were part of the Progressive movement to use the power of government to solve social problems. It wasn't until after WWII that narcotic drug use became largely a vice of the urban poor, since prior to that the urban poor in America didn't have the disposable income to spend on expensive drugs (alcohol was much cheaper). Idle rich people using narcotics (as was largely the case 100 years ago, particularly among whites) didn't elicit the sympathy or call to action than the problem of poor people destroying their lives and their families' lives with drug use did in more recent times. Nowadays heroin addiction is a major social problem in dirt poor agrarian countries as well as in super wealthy industrialized ones.

http://www.stripes.com/news/middle-east/report-drug-use-plagues-millions-of-afghans-including-children-1.345742

A Darwinist's Crooked Slant on Society

E-mail To An Educator: An Appendix to War Drums

I recently received a complimentary e-mail from a teacher about my coverage of the Baltimore Purge, in which she mentioned a donation to a political candidate she regards as potentially useful in eliminating the inequity that seems to have powered the recent unrest. I answered with the following missive.

For me, anybody who gets elected that is off of the main Liberal-conservative axis is a good thing.

To me, the Baltimore Purge/Riot was a war story, about an under strength army of occupation getting embarrassed and bloodied by a restive underclass. And yet this still feeds the political elite, as most of these stupid working class and middle class whites sided with the cops because they knew people who were being attacked by blacks, and never made the connection that they were being attacked by blacks because the blacks think the white population supports the cops that are attacking them!

So what do they do, they support the police, and the brutal youth gangs continue to attack individuals of the population that they see as supportive of their enemy—the police. It seems a nice tidy cycle to me.

Both the black and whites are so stupid they can be kept forever at each other's throats and backs to the good of the government who gains strength every time it is called upon to act from either side. In the end I think that people deserve oppressive governance due to their stupidity. I also think that each one of our disastrous presidents [Carter was the only decent man to hold office in my life time, and he was a fool, helpless before the skullduggery of his handlers.] is the president that the American People deserve at that time. Electoral politics is a genius gambit, because it permits the majority to choose the rulers, and the majority—I'm sure you know better than I, you being a teacher—is necessarily the most ignorant slice of the population. [Let's not drag the retards into this.] Hence our idiot legions elect politicians that have engaged in war more frequently than the Romans or the Mongols, and have managed to kill even more people. So, my interest in electoral politics is similar to my interest in medieval military logistics, a morbid study of the nuts, bolts, gears and bowels of a killing machine.

I was pleased that the State's Attorney did not prosecute curfew arrest victims.

Aljazeera America had a nice Fault Line piece on Baltimore filmed just before the riots which was eye opening. To see the bimbo mayor announcing the decline of crime in Baltimore on the eve of the purge riots was just precious.

Speaking of the mayor, I was at Jimmy's diner in Fells Point on Sunday, when I saw a glamour photo of the mayor on the boxed in pillar next to my table. In marker, on the bottom corner, she had scrawled, I Love Jimmy's.

I was of a mind to take the framed photo and place it above the mattress on the floor of my man cave, but was dissuaded by my Sister Terry, who actually slapped me. My mother commented that the apostrophe at the end of Jimmy would make the picture worthless as a sexual trophy. I countered that it would be up to the viewer's imagination as to what possession of mine the declaration addressed. Oh well.

The Wedge Formation
How Could the Pigs Not Get Their Ass Kicked So Badly the Next Time? A Man Question from Steevo

"Dude, I hate pigs, and I hate these ghetto motherfuckers. So next time I'd like to see the pigs at least get their licks in. How can they suck so totally with that riot gear? How could the pigs not get their ass kicked so badly the next time? And also, would you be willing to train 'em?"

Steevo

For the record I despise the police and the ghetto hoodrats they battle, so Steevo and I are on the same page there. I would not work for a gang, nor would I work for something even more corrupt, such as a police department. However, if individuals, or even pairs or trios of cops or gang bangers came to me looking for riot instruction I would coach them, at no charge, because I don't take dirty money knowingly. [I did recently take $80 from a former police supervisor who is now a practicing lawyer, for a consultation.]

Why?

In my mind combat bestows virtue on the otherwise un-virtuous. Indeed, the term virtue comes from the Latin virtus. Which basically means 'prepared to kick your hairy barbarian ass, so that I can enjoy your woman's soft barbarian ass.'

High-minded ethical concerns out of the way, what would the training look like?

I have included a street level video below which you may use a reference. Incidentally, in the video below the cops fought like squeamish Aztecs and the hoodrats fought like conquistadors did when they were outnumbered.

277

Gear

The police riot gear sucks. Realizing that most cops are wimps and will be tossed shit equipment and remain untrained in close combat, I suggest that athletic cops train up on their own as strike teams, replacing the following crappy equipment with the real deal.

1. Worst of all is the helmet. A real riot busting cop needs to be wearing a hockey helmet with full face cage. Just buy whatever the PBR studs are wearing.

2. Riot shields suck! I once destroyed a riot shield of the round German police design that is better than what we see these cops using on TV. I smashed that shield up with a rattan stick while fighting Big Robert Gyer in about 1 minute. I suggest Cold Steel or another brand of polyethylene shields for small shields on the strike teams. For large strike team shields use the ballistic door-crashing shields usually wasted on crashing in some ghetto door. We have made our own shields from a polyethylene oil drum barrel, and they are almost indestructible, even against steel. The top and bottom make two bucklers and the body makes two Roman scutum-style body shields.

278

3. Asp batons, in evidence in the accompanying video, always fail on contact and rarely stop active aggressors. Keep that thing on your belt for a back up or for breaking windows.

4. Traditional police batons are okay, but a little short and a little too likely to crack a skull, and the last thing a Baltimore cop needs is a dead hoodrat carcass on his hands. Cops who are stuck with the crappy riot shield should use these.

5. Riot sticks were designed to be wielded from horseback, using the horse's body mass. On foot the reach is largely wasted. Riot sticks on foot should be used like a two handed sword, as all but heavyweight stick fighters are going to lack the forearm strength to use this weapon with dexterity with one hand. Give your biggest men riot sticks and increased body armor—base ball shins and lacrosse shoulders—and use them as part of a four man team, discussed in tactics below.

6. Rattan sticks of ¾ inch thickness and 28 inches in length, with carved butts should be used by any hand to hand effectives other than the big boys with the riot sticks. They handle better, break less often, break less bones, and shock more soft tissue than traditional hard wood batons.

Skills

The following skills are equally required and can be taught up to effect in 1 hour sets, taking 24 hours to reach a self-trainable level of competence for most fighters.

1. Stick stroking

2. Stick retention

3. Shield use

4. Mobility

Below is a link on stick stroking in which Charles and I hit the bag with rattan sticks, with body mechanics explained in the accompanying text.

Bag Work

Tactics

Against lateral formations like the shield wall used by the cops and the open skirmishing swarm used by the hoodrats, the wedge formation works equally well, and was deployed by Macedonian and Norman horseman, who were renown for dealing death blows to light and heavy troops alike. As with any combat victory goes to he who dominates the combat space and that is more about mobility than anything.

The basic Norman configuration was three troopers in a wedge. As our hood rat and cop forces will not be slashing and stabbing with swords and lances and continuing on by, but are focused on looting and taking prisoners, I have various recommendations for the two sides.

1. The cops should place a big armored man with riot stick in the open end of the three man wedge, with the objective of the three men in the wedge to be largely getting his big ass on the target. The wedge itself should form up first with a point man with a large shield, and second by left flanker with a small shield. This guy should be your best stick.

2. The right wing of the wedge should be held by a left hander, or a right hander trained to use a shield in his right hand. He is the formation maintenance guy. The problem with shield-based formations is a tendency to drift to the right behind the next soldier's shield [held in his left hand], with the last guy on the right, not having cover on the flank, and edging toward whatever covering terrain there is.

The right flanker should keep his hand empty and on the point man's back. He would be the officer as well, with an asp on his belt. This four man team has two dedicated shield men who should move offensively, and two dedicated stick strikers who would use the cover of the point and right flanker as a base of operations.

3. Unit tactics with cop wedges are flexible, and should be based on three wedges ranging out to the front and flanks of a shield wall, instead of these slacker cops wandering around the backfield as seen on the video. The shield wall should shield a medical team, so that casualties do not have to be dragged a significant distance. There should be a four man rear guard armed with beanbag shotguns to make certain there is no overrun, and for use in dealing with rooftop threats.

4. Your operational cop riot unit should consist of 1 20-person static shield wall, two medics and two commanding officers behind the wall, a 4-man rear guard, and three 4-man wedges, for a total of 40 persons, only 12 of whom need be combat qualified with the stick and shield, the rest operating in a support role.

5. For you hoodrats I suggest the same 4-man wedge formation, with three dudes with trash can lids and bats forming the point and flanks of the wedge and one dude, with a real good throwing arm, armed with a first baseman's mitt for catching whatever the cops might throw back his way. He should not have to carry his ammo. I recommend that the point man and flankers each have a backpack full of ammo: halved bricks to hit the shield wall, lacrosse balls and stones to harass cops who actually have balls, and whole bricks to bust up hard-headed pigs.

I stand willing to coach either side, and even referee organized skirmishes. Have at it, and please, try to do better than this. I don't want to give those boys in Kiev an excuse to laugh at our rioting and counter rioting methods the next time.

Peace is for pussies.

https://www.youtube.com/watch?v=qFzjkNkVcPU

Massivewax   May 18, 2015 6:39 PM EDT

James,

Why do you feel that asp batons always fail? The video doesn't really depict any melee attacks with them.

I have one of my own, and although I've never had a need to use it on an attacker, it always has seemed particularly brutal to me, like it could easily break bones. After reading your comment, I did a search and the only think I could find was an LEO forum saying the same thing that you did. From a tactical standpoint, why don't they pass the test? How have you seen them used (poorly) against attackers?

responds: May 19, 2015 2:11 PM EDT

I have interviewed two cops who have used them, and in both instances they failed to stop the suspect, and bent like a coat hanger. Also, in Loren Christianson's book on skinhead street gangs he describes a West Coast cop bending his asp over a skinheads cranium, which did not stop said skinhead.

I have fought with 1/2 inch aluminum

rods and 1 1/4 inch steel pipes—
actually lost most of those—and can
attest that the flesh shock is nothing
compared to rattan, and the bone
damage is no worse than oak. Metal
needs to be heavy to work as a blunt
object. You want a bar, not a pipe, if
you are crippling someone. The ASP is
essentially a pipe. I recommend it as a
weapon for tight spots like doorways,
halls and restrooms. It is handy for
breaking and entering. I could make it
work, since I've had over 600 stick
fights, and am a good hand sniper, but
would prefer something more reliable.

The one time the asp has been used
effectively was against a knife, paired
with a smock [cloth work garment].
But the knifer was behaving
ineffectively, and Mister Kenneth was
in a chump stomping mood. If you are
going to use the ASP strike the hands
and the ear [this could kill, even with
this piece of junk so don't do it
casually]. Do not come down on the
head, and you are probably wasting
your time on the shoulder unless the
dude is a bone rack. It is better than
nothing, and recommended primarily

because it is easy to carry and deploy.

The bad legal point is that this metal telescopic baton will punch a hole in a head—which could be bad legal news for the wielder. Also, it does not have the mass to impart sufficient shock, and it is the shock that stops, not the cracked bone. Functionally I do not trust the thing for a thrust, and suspect it might collapse.

This summer I promise to gather various blunt implements and test them on video. And please, don't even thing about using the spring action ASP.

Jeremy Bentham   May 14, 2015 3:05 PM EDT

"An army of deer led by a lion is more to be feared than an army of lions led by a deer."

Chabrias, Athenian General, 4th century B.C.

Another thing we must keep in mind in our discussion of tactics is the importance of effective leadership and the aggressive will to win to the successful conduct of any conflict. That was sorely lacking on the part of the Baltimore police and the individual police officers suffered defeat and

humiliation on account of it. The political
leadership of Baltimore did not want to win the
fight against the rioters; it didn't advance their
hidden agenda to suppress the urban unrest.
Remember that the police were told to "stand
down", to not seek to disperse or defeat the rioters,
to merely contain the protest/riot. So that is what
the cops did. Deprived of the authority and ability
to take to fight to the enemy, they adopted defeatist
tactics. Tactics intended merely to help avoid injury
to themselves while "containing" the disorder. They
stood in a line with shields and made themselves
targets for the brick throwing hoodrats.

Presumably the cops were to maintain this posture
until the hoodrats grew weary of the game and
went home. The last thing the city leaders wanted
was for the police to "win ugly". In their minds they
did not want to have to look at video of cops
clubbing down protesters with wild abandon... you
know like in Chicago 1968. The Woman didn't care
that this excessively passive posture made the
police to look like incompetent, impotent fools. The
Woman hates all cops and soldiers on general
principles anyway. Even the ones that serve her. So
if any of those jingoistic myrmidons end up looking
like goofs while carrying out Her wishes, so fucking
what?!

responds: May 16, 2015 6:27 PM EDT

I know I'm hard on the cops.

Seeing this video really made me feel bad for the cops that got hurt, who had been failed at every level by their leadership.

Fatmanjudo   May 13, 2015 7:29 PM EDT

You forgot the most important member of the police formation without whom it would never work—the Cheka officer to shoot those who abandon the formation. Average, non- swat cops are trained to never fight fair, so what you are describing goes against all their training.

responds: May 16, 2015 6:35 PM EDT

Let's compromise and have me beat them across the back with a rattan rod. I'd love to be a Centurian, if just for one day.

Jeremy Bentham   May 13, 2015 4:23 PM EDT

Don't forget the scoops...The scoops are on the way!

http://www.bing.com/videos/search?q=soylent+gr
een+the+scoops+are+on+the+way&FORM=VIRE4#
view=detail&mid=CB8D5513251EDDB1599CCB8D
5513251EDDB1599C

> **responds:** May 16, 2015 6:36 PM EDT
> Thank for that heads up Jeremy.
> I would dearly love to see hoodrats
> scooped up like milk duds at an old
> time candy counter...

The End, until the next Harm City Purge